LETTERS FROM LAGOS

MAUREEN HANSON

DEDICATION

For my Grandchildren

ACKNOWLEDGEMENT

My thanks go to friends and family, who encouraged me, with gentle persuasion, to start writing about our life in Nigeria.

To Mike and Janey Wilson, who hold wonderful 'Creative Writing' courses in Castillon La Bataille, nr. Bordeaux, and where I met many lovely Authors who use it regularly as a retreat, and others, who like me, were inspired by their encouragement to continue to write. Many thanks.

Thankyou also to Carmelina Hancock, who lived in Lagos in the 1970's, and kindly read through the first draft and corrected many mistakes I had made.

For their infinite patience, their own memories and their vast computer skills, without which I could not have reached even half of this stage in my memoirs, my enormous gratitude goes to Sally and Nick.

To Danielle Hanson who has created the beautiful cover for the book.

To all our friends who are mentioned in our story, 'Thanks for the Memories' and for making what could have been a pretty difficult posting, into one that has had such a lasting impression on all our family's lives. You became part of our 'family' and we have a friendship which has lasted like no other.

Finally, to Brian, who seized the opportunity to move to Nigeria in the first place. Without you, none of our 'adventures' would have happened. You had all the trials and tribulations of every day at the office to contend with, as well as the frustrations of travelling to and fro on the roads and in the air. You worked so hard under trying and frustrating circumstances but somehow we always managed to have alot of fun along the way.

Thank you also for your enormous help and patience on reading through every passage I wrote and discussing all the finer details with me at length.

I hope it brought back some good memories for you too.

CONTENTS

PROLOGUE

A short time before my Mother died, she handed me an old carrier bag which was stuffed full of letters. 'There you are' she said, 'I kept all the letters you wrote to us from Nigeria. Perhaps you can find the time to write a book one day!'

I took them home with me, and the next day, I selected one of the letters at random.   It had been some twenty years since we had lived in Nigeria and we now had busy lives back in the UK. That letter brought back so many memories but for some reason, I couldn't bring myself to read any more.

 I stuffed it back into the bag and pushed it to the back of the wardrobe where it remained until many years later when we retired and moved to France. Once we had settled into our new home, I took them out again and finally started to read them all.

CHAPTER 1 - APRIL 1986

It was pitch dark in the 'bush.' The moon hadn't yet risen and the only light came from the headlights as we crawled along the tarmac strip that ran down the middle of the rough road. A huge Mann Diesel lorry towing an equally long trailer blasted his strident, blaringly loud, air-horn, forcing us off the metal strip onto the laterite as he thundered past us at enormous speed. All went quiet again, save for the low revs from the engine of the Range Rover we were travelling in and the sounds of the hot tropical night that drifted in through the open windows. Brian was driving very slowly.

We had just had our fourth puncture of the day on what had become a nightmare journey of some 450 miles that he had driven from Lagos towards Abuja, a new capital city that was being developed in central Nigeria. We had no more spare tyres with us. It had become impossible to buy any in Nigeria but it was essential that we reached Abuja that night. Brian and his colleague Paul, who was with us in the car, had important meetings with the Minister of Development for the new capital the next morning and we should have been off the road and in our hotel long before dark. If it hadn't been for all the punctures we had experienced on the way we would have been. So we couldn't stop. It definitely wasn't safe to be driving here on the roads at night. Highway robberies were commonplace and reports in the newspapers every day told stories of people who had been held up at gunpoint, robbed, and in some cases hacked to death by the felons, if they had tried to defend themselves. The robbers, who then mysteriously disappeared into the night, never to be found or brought to justice, just continued their ghastly trade unimpeded.

We were bumping along on what was left of the tyres, running on the rim of the punctured one by this time. The atmosphere in the car was really tense, nobody spoke, as mile after slow mile we kept trundling along hoping and praying that surely, nothing worse could possibly befall us this night.

But it did. Suddenly, out of the darkness ahead, a light started flashing at us indicating that we should pull over to the side of the road. Brian had no option but to continue driving slowly towards it. The light kept on flashing, insistently trying to direct us off the road. Brian wouldn't stop because there was only dense bush on either side of us and who knows what dangers might have been lurking in there.

As we drew alongside the light, a man clad only in a loin cloth jumped out and started to jog alongside the car. My mouth went dry, and my heart started to pound loudly in my chest. Even in the heat of the tropical night I broke out into a cold sweat and started to shake with fright. We could only see the whites of his eyes as he stared in at us through the open windows. Then he spoke. 'Good evening Baturi' he said. 'I go pass you on the road. I see you are in trouble. I wait for you now!' Brian kept on driving as fast as he dared to go. The man continued to jog along beside us as he demanded 'Where are you going Baturi?' 'We have to get to Abuja tonight' said Brian. 'Aaha! You no go get dere dis night' said the man. My heart beat even faster. 'Make you go come with me now' he said. 'I be the Chief of the village dere. You go come with me now now and I go help you.' We looked over to where he was pointing and saw the glow of firelight deep in the bush. What were we to do? It was becoming obvious that we would never make it to Abuja due to the state of our vehicle. 'Can you get us a taxi or transport of some kind?' asked Brian. 'Yes, yes, you go come with me now and I get you taxi' the man said. With that, he darted across the road in front of the car and ran down a cutting through the bush, heading towards the light from the fire. 'Shall we follow?' asked Brian. We didn't have much choice. Better to go and see what was in the village than to spend the night on a deserted road miles from anywhere where we could have been waylaid by robbers, or worse. We turned off the road and bumped down a rough track,

6

following the man until we drew up in a clearing, where the fire was burning brightly.   The fire was surrounded by a ring of thatched mud huts.

This was the village!

Nobody else was around but the sound of our vehicle arriving soon brought curious faces peering out of the doorways, lit up like burnished copper from the reflected glow of the fire.

Several men came over to have a closer look at us.   The man we had followed was speaking rapidly and making excited gestures to the other men who now surrounded our car.   We could not understand what they were saying as it was in their own tribal language.   My fears grew stronger. What was going to happen to us now?   Terrible thoughts crowded through my mind.   What were we even doing here? Our children were in England! They might never find out what had become of us. We might never be found. Would I be tied up and raped? Would they hack us all to death with machetes?   What fate had even brought us to this point in our lives?

CHAPTER 2 - DEPARTURE & ARRIVAL
1970

'Are we in Africa yet?' asked Nicholas aged five, as we began our descent into London's Heathrow Airport. We had left Manchester, Ringway Airport some forty minutes earlier on Friday 4th September 1970 when we had waved goodbye to my parents, my brother and sister and their families, who had all come to see us off on this first step of our adventure to the 'great unknown.'

My husband, Brian, had taken a job in Nigeria with Pfizer Pharmaceuticals Inc. They had an Agricultural Division in Ikeja near Lagos and they owned and controlled several mills throughout West Africa, which manufactured animal feeds and veterinary products. This was in addition to their pharmaceutical products which were manufactured worldwide.

Brian had gone out to Nigeria several weeks before us, which was the policy of most companies in those days, primarily to see if the new employee was able to adapt to the climate, the working conditions, the people and the huge culture shock, before going to the enormous expense of moving and housing a whole family out in Nigeria. Brian had obviously 'passed muster' because here we were on a warm, late summer evening, on our first flight. I was twenty-nine years old, our daughter Sally was nine and our son Nicholas was five.

It had all been very hectic and exciting until then. Packing up, sorting out the house and storing the furniture. Trying to decide what clothes we would need when we had absolutely no realization of what the climate was really like. Travelling to Liverpool to sort out our passports and entry permits. Having to have vaccinations for smallpox, yellow fever, typhoid, para-typhoid A and B vaccine, cholera, etc. Last minute trips to the dentist, hairdresser, and various friends and family. Then came the moment when we had to say 'goodbye' at the airport and the children and I set off on a lonely walk down one of the legs to the airplane which was waiting on the tarmac.

I remember looking back with a huge lump in my throat, trying not to let the children see the tears in my eyes just before we boarded the plane. My mother and father and all the family were pressed up against the enormous glass window at Ringway Airport, waving 'goodbye' to us before we finally disappeared into the plane's interior.

The plane was mostly full of businessmen returning to London but the air hostess who greeted us at the top of the steps said that she had noticed us in the departure lounge and had kept three seats together for us. The children had a carrier bag each with books, colouring pencils and a few little toys to keep them occupied on what was to be a seven hour onward flight to Nigeria from London.

The stewardess had noticed a gun sticking out of the top of Nicholas' bag! It was only a plastic one but had a long muzzle and made quite a realistic rat-a-tat noise like a machine gun when you pulled the trigger! She took the bag off him and said it was best to keep it safely in the Captain's cabin until we reached our destination! In those days it had never occurred to me that it might be considered suspicious. If it happened now, we would probably have caused a severe panic and immediate evacuation of the plane!

At Heathrow, we had a few hours to wait before boarding a VC10 BOAC jet to Lagos Ikeja Airport. I had to try to work out where we needed to be in order to get on our flight, as flying and airports were a totally new experience for us. We sat in front of the information chart, waiting for it to say when our flight was boarding, hardly daring to take our eyes off it. Technology was not then as advanced as it is today and we were only informed when to go to the departure lounge by watching the board for our flight number to click into place.

On a quick visit to the toilets with the children, I noticed another young woman with a very tiny newborn baby. She was changing it's nappy on a pad in the ladies' room, while her three other children, who seemed to be similar in age to ours, hovered round. I was so relieved to find, when our flight was finally called, that they were actually going on the same plane as we were. This plane was huge in comparison to the one we had just flown in from Manchester to London and I didn't see much of that family again once we were on board, as they were seated at the front of the plane and we were half-way back.

We had only had a light snack at Heathrow, as we understood that a meal would be served on the flight. As the flight was late taking off, it was nearly midnight, the Captain announced as soon as we were airborne that he was going to keep the lights in the cabin switched off in order to allow all the children, and those others who wanted to sleep, to settle down before the food was served. Nicky was hungry, but also very tired by then and happily slept soon after take-off. Sally managed to stay awake for the meal, before she too finally fell asleep.

I was far too excited to sleep and didn't want to miss anything that was happening in the cabin all night. There were no in-flight films in those days so not very much was going on. The cabin roof of the VC10 had a wonderful feature of the night sky lit by the stars. When the main cabin lights were out, it gave one an amazing feeling of really flying through time and space.

It was a very long night. I wondered what my family were thinking now back at home. Were they wondering, like me, what our new life was going to be like? Had we done the right thing in uprooting our children and taking them halfway across the world to an unknown destination? It wasn't as if we could visit every weekend. We would be stuck there for at least ten months before we could come back home again. Would they miss us? Even worse, how much would we miss them? The international telephone system hadn't yet been set up, and apparently the local telephones were pretty useless. The terrible war in Biafra was only just finishing and times were very hard for Nigeria and its people.

From time to time I peered down through the small window of the plane and saw vast acres of dusty brown wasteland punctuated here and there by darker shapes. It seemed to go on forever.   The flight was due to take seven hours but because it was all new to me and with my mounting trepidation and excitement, I just couldn't settle down to sleep. Gradually the darkness lightened and turned to a misty rose; the new dawn was breaking. We flew ever onwards as the sky became golden orange and the blood-red rays of the rising sun glinted on the wings of the aircraft. The dark shapes in the desert below us now became large mountains and escarpments as the sunlight touched the ground and turned to gold.

We finally began our descent to Kano Airport, a major town in Northern Nigeria. As we dropped ever lower I could see that the houses were all square-shaped and seemed to be built mainly of baked earth. There were huge and weird-shaped trees with enormous trunks and short, stubby branches that almost looked as if the trees had been planted upside down and the roots were sticking out of the top. Later, I found out that these were the ancient Baobab trees, sometimes known as 'the Tree of Life' and had seemingly been on Earth since time immemorial. The time in the plane was now somewhere around six o'clock and already the sun was hot and the sky dazzlingly clear in the early morning light.

We had to stay on the plane as we had only stopped to pick up some passengers on their way to Lagos. Nick awoke as we landed and was annoyed to find that he had missed his breakfast, which had been served earlier before we landed in Kano. He had to wait until we took off for Lagos before he was offered a cold platter of garlic sausage, hard boiled egg, anchovy and olives! This was all that was being served during the short onward flight. Definitely not the sort of fare that a five-year-old English boy was used to eating for breakfast!

As we prepared for take off again and the plane's doors were closed at Kano Airport the air hostess, who wore white gloves as part of her uniform in those days, walked down the aisle of the plane with a large aerosol can of insect killer in each hand. She proceeded to spray over the passengers from one end of the plane to the other and then back again, leaving all the passengers coughing and choking in her wake! This was our first taste of what it would be like from now on to keep the deadly mosquito at bay!

Sally and Nick were getting very excited and couldn't wait to land now and see their Daddy again.

The children of the lady at the front of the plane had obviously woken up and felt the same, as they decided to take a walk up and down the aisle. They obviously remembered seeing Sally and Nick at the Airport at Heathrow and they all eyed each other up and down, as children do! I saw their mother standing up to take the baby out of the tiny cot that was slung above the bulwark seat, she looked exhausted. I felt very sorry for her as I had heard her baby crying throughout most of the night. She obviously hadn't had much sleep either. I thanked my lucky stars that my children had been able to sleep on most of that long flight.

The landscape changed again as we flew south, from the dry desert of the North, through the Savannah regions and on to the tropical climate of Lagos. My first memory as we descended towards Ikeja Airport, was of myriads of palm trees covering the ground and of the rusty red corrugated iron roofs on all the houses. We tried to see out of the small windows of the plane as the pilot found the runway and landed with an almighty bump before the air brakes slammed us forward into our fastened seat belts and a loud burst of spontaneous clapping erupted from all the Nigerian passengers who had joined the flight from Kano.

We had finally arrived.

Livestock FeedsLtd.
PMB 1097 Ikeja.
Lagos State
Nigeria

Sept 7th.1970

Dearest Mum and Dad.
Hope you and all the family are well. We are fine, and as you can see from the above address, have arrived safely after a very long but thankfully, uneventful flight. Sally and Nicholas coped well and in spite of mounting excitement, managed to sleep most of the way once we took off from Heathrow Airport. After seven hours, we finally landed at Lagos Ikeja Airport. There are only two runways here. The main runway is for all the international flights and a much smaller one is for the domestic ones. When we landed, I saw through the window a flight of steps was being wheeled across the tarmac with rather too much enthusiasm by several Nigerian workers who were pushing it towards the plane. They failed to stop it in time and crashed it into the side of the plane, which delayed our disembarkation somewhat, as the buckled steps then had to be repaired before we were allowed to get off! It was quite funny really!

When we finally left the cool air-conditioning of the plane's interior, nothing had prepared us for the sheer wall of heat and humidity that threatened to suffocate us as we walked across the tarmac and into the small building that is the airport terminal here. I have to say, it was quite bewildering and frightening to be thrust into the turmoil and pandemonium that followed. The small hut was filled to capacity, not only with passengers, but also with what seemed like several hundreds of Nigerians. Some of them were in uniforms and others were in their native dress, but all seemed to be shouting, "Master! Master,'or "Madam Psst! Madam!" Hundreds more seemed to be crowded outside, shouting through the openwork breeze block walls, some even climbing up them to get a better view of the arriving passengers. It was complete chaos and noise with everyone pushing and shoving but with no notices anywhere to tell us where to go.

I had noticed a lady and her four children in the airport at Heathrow while we were waiting for our flight, and had been pleased to see that she was also getting on the same flight as us to Lagos. Amid the chaos in the arrivals hall, I noticed her again, being warmly greeted by her husband who was flanked by two Nigerians who were escorting them all through the pushing throngs to a desk at the far end. I looked frantically around, in vain, for Brian while trying to stop several Nigerians from trying to grab our passports. I later discovered that one had been hired by Brian to try and help us through the airport. They are known as 'fixers' who oil the wheels of passage through Immigration, Health and Passport control if you 'grease their palms' with 'dash,'as it is called here, or money. They are known at the airport and used by the travel agents to help poor unsuspecting innocents like me, to get through the chaos.   Unfortunately, I didn't know this at the time and thought he was trying to steal our passports!

I fought my way through the crowd to the desk trying to keep the children with me.   Sweat was pouring off us by this time. We had on entirely the wrong clothes for this climate.   A crimplene dress and padded anorak are definitely not appropriate out here in this heat and humidity!   The children at last spotted Brian who was trying to peer in through the open block walls from outside. We finally got through the passport control desk and answered all the questions about why we were here.   We then reached the luggage collection point and after watching all the baggage go round and round on the moving belt and waiting for what seemed like hours, discovered that one of our cases was missing!   Finally, and thankfully, Brain was allowed in to help us.   It was so fantastic for us all to be together again at last.   He called an expatriate manager who worked for the airline that we had travelled on, and he assured us that they would do everything possible to get our case restored to us in the fastest possible time.

What a relief it was to leave that airport with all the noise and chaos behind.   Unfortunately, the road from the airport was also thronged with people *and traffic. Battered cars, and taxis, which are mainly old Morris Minors, were driving far too fast and frighteningly, overtaking us on both sides! Most amazing of all are the Mammy Wagons. These are old five ton Bedford truck chassis with brightly coloured slatted wooden bodies, built rather like a four poster bed with seats all the way round the inside. They are open at the sides and rear and were filled to capacity with Nigerians who were also hanging on precariously from the sides and back. Their loads, or baggage, were piled high on the roof together with any livestock, which they happened to be transporting.*

In abundance also were adapted VW camper-type vans which are used as taxis and have been kitted out with as many seats as they can cram in. They are known locally as Kier-Kiers. I've never seen so many people in all my life. Even the train that we passed was choc-a-bloc full of people both inside and out; those who were outside, were clinging somewhat perilously to the window frames, which had no glass in them, and lots of people were even lying on the roof!

The roads are gutted all along with huge potholes and there are deep storm drains or open sewers on either side. The Mammy Wagons career at dangerously high speeds down the centre of the roads wherever possible, playing 'chicken' with any other car, bicycle, or people, to see who will be the first to swerve over on to the dusty red laterite strip that borders each side of the mangled tarmac. On some of the Mammy Wagons a live monkey sits on the top, chained to the vehicle. I think it's supposed to be a sort of lucky talisman.

Apparently there are frequent and horrendous crashes, as these vehicles are never well maintained and are always tremendously overloaded. I noticed that they also have many very profound sayings written over the top of the driver's compartments, such as "Christ Almighty' or "No condition is permanent' which I find very amusing and are also highly appropriate I should imagine!

Along each side of the road there are mud huts with tin roofs, or just a simple construction with a palm thatch providing shade, outside which the women and children sit with huge woven baskets or large trays full of wares such as bright red tomatoes, potatoes, sweet corn, plantains and green citrus fruits. Some have tins of sardines stacked on the trays and Tomapep, which is an extraordinarily hot tomato and pepper puree, which I'm told finds its way into most Nigerian cooking pots. Cigarettes named Target or Bicycle are sold singly, or by the 'stick' for one penny each. Matches and groundnuts are also on every tray. Every now and again we passed huts that were selling such things as electrical goods, from where really loud music was blaring forth, obviously in an effort to prove that they had the biggest and the best stereo and speakers on the market. The young children outside were dancing to the rhythmical beat of the "Highlife' and waved happily calling out "Oyinbo' as we passed. "Oyinbo'I found out, is a Yoruba word that means light skin, referring to white people or even albino Nigerians.

There is a rhyme that the children sing referring to the belief that if you eat hot peppers your skin will become darker in colour, and you won't look quite so odd, which is obviously how the Nigerians see us.

Rubber tyres were in abundance at stalls along the roadside, both car and bicycle tyres. Children ran merrily along bowling old bicycle tyres or the old rims, as if they were hoops. Some of the huts are full of cotton materials with extremely colorful African designs all over them. These are the materials from which the men and women make their clothes. Some of the wealthier families have their own ' cloth' or design, which all the family wear. It is quite strange to see several women walking along together all wearing the same things. The elaborate head ties and blouses of the wealthy women are made from exquisite lace, usually brought in from Switzerland, in matching or contrasting colours. The men wear elaborate robes too, with much embroidery around the neckline and sleeve ends. They usually have intricately embroidered headgear to match. The market women and the poorer men, on the other hand, wear only simple wraps from their waists or the men have a type of pyjama suit, or Agbada, in simple cotton. The market womens' head tie is normally a purely functional length of cloth which is tied around in a circle and assists them when they balance their huge loads or baskets of wares on the tops of their heads. It is quite amazing to see them, able to walk along so gracefully with an enormous basket full of goods on their heads and usually with a baby, or 'Piccin,' tied onto their backs with yet another length of 'cloth.' Both the mothers and their babies seem very happy with this arrangement and you rarely hear babies crying. I suppose the close proximity and constant movement of the Mother is akin to the baby still being in the womb.

As we drove on I noticed some of the women sitting on the side of the road with a small cooking pot over a fire. Sometimes we passed what looked like huge bananas being grilled over the embers, these are plantains, and the women sell their food wrapped up in a banana leaf. Often we passed women grinding maize or cassava in a huge wooden bowl. Two women stand either side of the bowl, each holding a long pole, which they take in turns to pound rhythmically and very energetically one to the other until the grains are ground to flour.

We entered the comparative quiet of the GRA, Government Residential Area, where most of the expatriates live. Here, thankfully, there are no traders or public transport so the roads are quieter, cleaner and more orderly. Large houses stand in large gardens, or 'compounds' as they are known here, usually planted with trees and tropical plants of brilliant hues. Most of the houses are painted cream or white which was fairly dazzling in the intense sunlight. The heat by this time, which was nearly midday, was almost overpowering.

We swept through the double gates of a semi-circular driveway and drew up in front of the wide steps that led up to the front door of a large bungalow.

21

This is our home!   Our steward, Francis and the gardener, Israel Achilefu, came out to greet us.   They both live in the small quarters which are situated in the compound of our house.   Israel with his wife Grace and two small children.   Francis is a young single man. We also have a 'night watchman' called David.   He arrives every evening when it goes dark and sits by the gate on a sheet of cardboard, or in the car port, or on the veranda, where I suspect he sleeps, until morning.

The house is fantastic.   It is a large sprawling bungalow with a covered veranda at the front and the back.   You enter through double paned glass doors into a very large L-shaped lounge and dining room with a very convenient drinks bar in the angle of the L-shape. Dad, you would love that wouldn't you?   The kitchen is large and airy with a laundry room at the back containing two very deep stone sinks.   No washing machines here I'm afraid!   There are three large bedrooms and two bathrooms plus an extra cloakroom situated off the lounge.   All the large windows in every room which are protected with ornate wrought iron bars, known locally as 'teef-bars' are thrown open to catch any possible movement of air.   There is one small Carrier air conditioning unit in the outside wall of each bedroom and we only use these at night.

The furniture is pretty non-existent and rudimentary.   All we have at the moment is one dining table, six chairs, one settee on 'stick-like legs' with square foam cushions for the seats and chair backs.   There are two or three armchairs, which are

22

'old colonial style', with foam squares to make seats and chair backs, much like the settee. These have the annoying habit of all splitting up and moving around whenever anyone sits on them. Can't wait to get rid of them and find something more comfortable! The vast floors are grey and white Terrazzo with not a single rug or carpet square to be seen. Each bedroom has one bed in it. Thankfully, ours is at least a small double one!

There wasn't any food in the house to speak of and so after a coffee and a slice of toast, made from awful, sweet-tasting bread, Brian took us to the local store, which is called Kingsway. It was very hard to believe. There was hardly anything on the shelves. Of course it is very soon after the most horrendous Biafran War and indeed Brian told us that in some places in the East of the country, fighting is still continuing. He and one of his colleagues had been to the Livestock Feeds mill in Aba in the East and they had heard sporadic gunfire quite close to where they were staying during the evening. Very little is being imported at the moment and what is fresh is local. The meat counter made me heave, all it had on it were huge 'lumps' of indistinguishable meat. All of it seems to have been coloured the same red; beef, lamb or pork! It all looks the same to me. Brian said that the 'Expats' call the beef 'Fulani hump,' as you often see the herds of Fulani or Brahmin Cattle walking down from the North, shepherded by Northern tribesmen with their long white robes and large straw hats. The cattle have long curved horns and floppy ears and a hump at the back of the neck. By the time they have walked from the North down to Lagos, they have precious little meat left on their bones. Chicken was the only thing I could recognize but even they were thin and scrawny. There are no luscious, plump, oven-ready broilers like you have at home! Brian pointed out the boxes of frozen prawns that were local. He had already had some and said they were delicious, so we bought some of those. What we didn't know until later was that these are fished out of Lagos lagoon and that the very best and the biggest are caught under the bridge where the "night soil" is tipped after each nightly collection from the city! What I didn't know either, was that they had to be peeled and cooked! There is no fresh milk, butter or cheese. Only tins of powdered milk called Nido, which has to be reconstituted and tastes awful. Likewise, only tins of Blueband margarine, which is equally ghastly and sometimes rancid having been left on the shelves in the heat for too long. There are no biscuits, sauces, flavourings, marmalade or marmite and the bread all tastes sweet. Thank goodness coffee and tea is available! The sugar and flour are crawling with ants or weevils and have to be sifted before use. The only washing powder is Omo and the only household cleaner is Ajax or bleach. Well, at least we aren't spoilt for choice!

Brian took us outside to a stall on the roadside to buy fresh fruit and vegetables, which were equally sparse and strange looking. The woman selling them is known locally as 'sweaty Betty!' It was fairly obvious why. She was naked down to the waist and her empty *breasts hung elongated and flat against her front, obviously from long years of breast-feeding several children, some of whom were crawling around naked in the dirt by the stall.   Beads of sweat ran down her face and chest forming rivulets down her body until they reached the simple cotton wrap which was tied around her waist. From time to time she wiped it away with a large calloused hand or her cotton wrap. It was the first time I've ever had to buy anything from a half-naked person and I must say I was a bit surprised and embarrassed at first, but tried to appear as if it was the most normal thing in the world! The oranges, lemons and grapefruits all had green skins and looked unripe.   Brian assured me that they were alright inside. Mostly the oranges are squeezed for the juice, as all the citrus fruits here are full of pips.   The bananas, pineapples and paw-paw are also very green-looking but have to be very much part of our staple diet while we are living in Nigeria as there is little else. Avocado pears grow in abundance here and are therefore very cheap, which is fabulous because I love them.   The potatoes are all very small and the tomatoes are strangely segmented, looking rather like the inside of a mandarin orange, but at least these are red and very flavourful.   Small runner beans are always available it seems so I expect will become our most frequently eaten vegetable.   The lettuces are just like dandelion leaves, in fact I thought that was what they were when I first saw them.   The fruit and vegetables are like this because of the climate.   Even though it is usually very sunny, it is always so humid.*

I think the normal temperature is somewhere around 80° Fahrenheit and the humidity is also 80°. This apparently will vary somewhat during the rainy season and the dry.

The compound of our house is mostly lawn, though not a lawn as you know it. The grass is the sort that creeps along the top of the earth and will withstand the tropical climate to a degree. Apparently in the really dry season it all burns up but the minute the rains come along, it revives again.

There are two sets of double gates with a driveway that sweeps around in a semi-circle in front of the house. There is a small open stable on one side of the compound and the steward's quarters are alongside that. All along the front of the walls, which surround the compound, are tall Casuarina trees. Covering the veranda over the patio at the back of the house is a magnificent apricot-coloured bougainvillea tree, which is in full bloom right now and really gorgeous. There are several palm trees to one side, which produce delicious coconuts. The flesh inside is all soft and creamy, unlike any we have ever tasted before. Francis prepared some for the children and they loved it. We also have paw-paw trees and an avocado pear tree. The centre flowerbeds are full of beautiful brightly coloured red and orange canna lilies. Brian said that Israel our gardener had been working so hard to get this ready for our arrival. There are several bushes in the front garden that are full of beautiful bright red hibiscus blooms. The flowers on these bushes only last one day because of the heat and humidity, but there are always fresh ones blooming again the next day. One particularly beautiful bush by the front steps is known as a 'blushing hibiscus.' The reason for this being that the flowers on this bush are double ones and pure white when they open first thing in the morning. By the time evening comes, the blooms have turned to a beautiful deep pink colour. I soon learnt that a popular thing to do at dinner parties is to pick a single bloom first thing in the morning in its virginal stage and put it in the fridge. Just before guests arrive in the evening you float the beautiful flower in a large brandy goblet half full of water and during the dinner party the bloom will slowly turn to pink. Can't wait to try it!

I think that's enough for one letter. My hand is aching and sticking to the paper with the heat and humidity. Don't know how long this will take to reach you but just wanted you to know that we are here and everything is fine. Everything, that is except for the fact that our missing case hasn't yet been found and returned to us! It contained most of Nick's clothes, so the poor boy is forever having his shirt and pants whipped off him and washed. It is so hot here though that they soon dry!

Please could you let the rest of the family read this as I can't possibly write it all over again.

I'm really missing you all. Thank you so much for coming to the airport to see us off.

Will write again very soon. Lots of love to you all.

Maureen Brian Sally and Nicky. xxxx

Everything grew so quickly in the Lagos climate. We even had one tree in the compound, which seemed to go through the four seasons in two days. It was known as a shade tree because of its large leaves. Throughout Nigeria you would see people sitting, or more often, sleeping under its welcome shade in the middle of the day. Strangely enough, at a certain time each year, the large green leaves would suddenly turn red, curl up and fall off, all within a couple of days. The very next day, it would be sprouting new growth and at the end of the same week, would be in full leaf again.

The flame trees were also spectacular and the GRA had many avenues of these beautiful tall trees. As the name suggests, at blossom time, they looked to be on fire with the bright red pendulous flowers covering the canopy of green leaves. After they had flowered, the trees were covered with enormous dark brown seedpods which looked rather like giant broad beans. Another of my favourite trees in our compound was the frangipani, which had creamy white waxy blossoms, and smelled divine.

Livestock Feeds Ltd
PMB1097
IKEJA
Lagos State

Sept 1970

Dearest All

Hope all are well. We are fine, but just thought I would drop another line to tell you of all our doings since we arrived.

The children started school on Monday morning! The Grange school is situated right across the road from our house which is amazingly convenient! It is a private school and most of the British companies have debentures there. The headmistress is a British woman who is married to a Nigerian. Most of the teachers are British or Indian and there are also many Indian and Nigerian children there. Luckily Pfizer have five debentures and only three are being used at the moment, so both Sally and Nick could go. The children attend on five days a week from 8 o'clock in the morning until 12-30. There is no air-conditioning and it is considered too hot for the children to be able to concentrate in the afternoons so they come back home at lunch time which is lovely. The fees are £1.12.6d each per week. Apparently only the very wealthy Nigerians can afford

29

to send their children to the Grange school.   The
average wage of the stewards here is only £14.00 per
month. We find that hard to contemplate, but actually
for this, they normally live quite well, in a small house
in the compound where they work and where they are
able to house their family.   Our staff house has three
separate quarters which includes a basic toilet and
shower and running water.   This is shared between
Francis the steward, who has no family and Israel, the
gardener with his wife Grace and their two children.
They cook outside on an open fire for themselves.
Brian realised quite early on that they seemed to have
fairly free access to our food supplies and bar, but
reckons that as long as they don't abuse this privilege
too often, we should tend to turn a blind eye.

Early every morning, the cars start to come in
a steady stream down the road into the school opposite
us, dropping the children off and then continuing on,
out of the other gates at the far end.   At 7-55 am I
walked the children across the road and, somewhat
nervously, into the school. Would you believe it, the
first person I saw was the lady and her children who
had been on the plane with us. We practically fell into
each other's arms and greeted each other as though we
were long- lost friends. Her name is Rachel and her
husband Ken works for another pharmaceutical
company here too.   They live only a short distance
away from us in the GRA and we are able to walk to
each other's houses.   We went over to their house for
tea a couple of days ago and the children are all firm

friends already. Elizabeth is the same age as Sally and in the same class at school and the boys are Robert, who is two years younger than the girls and John who is about the same age as Nick. Rachel already has a nanny organised to look after their new baby Christina. It was so lovely to find that they are living close to us here.

All the children who go to the Grange school are aged between 5 and 10 years old. They have to be English speaking so they are mostly European pupils and teachers but there are quite a lot of Indian children as well and Nicholas has an Indian lady for his teacher. As I mentioned, only the wealthier Nigerian children go to the Grange, and some of them come from up to forty miles away every day. Mostly, they are the children of parents who have been educated themselves in British schools and who want their children to go on to study in UK at a later date. The children have lessons in the classrooms all morning with only one period for a break, so it is quite intense and very hot.

On the first morning, Sally found the sums were quite hard and she had to finish them before she was allowed out at playtime. By the time she got out to play, she had to go back in again for the next lesson! So you can imagine she wasn't too happy.

The French, Dutch, Lebanese and Germans usually have their own schools for their children. There is also a large American school in Lagos but of course they all follow their own country's curriculum.

The children of the local Nigerians go to large State primary and Secondary schools in the area. These seem to be based on the British State education system and most of the Nigerian people consider it to be vitally important to educate their children. All too many of them are desperately poor and illiterate and the children, therefore, have to go to work at an extremely early age, or resort to begging on the streets. If the children are educated and can get good jobs then they can look after the rest of the family. We've discovered that the 'extended family' system is still very much in operation here. Apparently, if a child of a village or a large family is chosen to be educated, the entire village or family will contribute to the funding of his education. When he finally gets a good job, he will be expected to 'look after' the family or village for the rest of his working days.

The children who go to the State schools all have a uniform, of sorts; it consists of a simple khaki-coloured cotton dress for the girls or shorts and shirt for the boys, which the local tailor makes up in a few hours. Most of the children don't even have shoes and the soles of their little feet are like leather. I think most of the teaching must be done from a blackboard as books are in short supply. You never see young children carrying any bags or satchels to school with them.

Situated next to the Grange school and therefore just a little way down from us on Harold Sodipo Crescent, is the Lagos Country Club. This consists of a building that contains a bar, a restaurant facility, though there is no restaurant now, and a large hall with a wooden floor which could be used for dancing. There is a stage at one end where the annual pantomime, films or amateur productions are staged. It has obviously had a far more glamorous past than it sports at the moment because it definitely looks very 'seedy' and past its best! Nevertheless, many expatriates, usually bachelors, have a reputation for 'hanging out' in the bar there every day after work, slowly getting sozzled and more morose as the evening wears on. Outside, there are tennis and squash courts and the gardens have obviously been laid out rather beautifully in the past, as there are beds of tropical flowers and colourful shrubs and palms. The grass in all the compounds is the variety that creeps along the surface, like Bermuda grass. Normal grass that grows lush and green in UK just would not survive the long dry periods of intense heat here.

There is a lovely swimming pool though, which seems to be quite well maintained, surrounded by many tables and chairs, with parasols to provide shade. The children and I have been to the pool after lunch nearly every day and we have quickly made friends with all the other mothers and children who do likewise. Sally is swimming like a fish already and Nicky won't be long. He jumps in even at the deep end, with his arm bands on and shows absolutely no fear whatsoever! It provides a welcome period for the children to exercise and 'let off steam' after a morning of concentration in the heat of the classroom.

The club also has several tennis and two squash courts. After Brian has gone to work, and the children to school every morning, I could hear the 'thwack- thwack' of the tennis balls from the courts across the road at the club. It wasn't very long before I was tempted to join them. I have met several new friends now and it's super to play a few sets before it gets too hot. The tennis courts are mainly red clay and have to be watered and swept after every set. We end up with our 'whites' covered in red dust so I was glad to have been told of a local tailor who will make up some tennis dresses for me if I give him one of mine to copy. I only brought one tennis dress out with me! You know they are 'tailors' by the way, because they walk around with an old-fashioned portable Singer sewing machine on their heads, just like Granny's old one that you gave me and hopefully, should be in our 'loads' somewhere on the high seas at this moment. I must say, I certainly wouldn't want to cart one of those around on my head all day!

Early mornings are glorious here. Dawn usually breaks at around about 6am and it is deliciously cool for an hour or so before the sun gets too hot. This is really the only time to play tennis, squash or golf if you don't want to expire in the heat. Darkness falls at around 7 o'clock every evening. This only varies slightly throughout the year according to the season. It is also quite good to play sports from about 5-30 onwards because the sun is going down by then. The nights never get cold and I am still finding it very strange to go out in the dark and realise that it is still hot and humid.

I love the wonderful sounds of the tropical nights which are so exciting. The crickets and cicadas provide a constant orchestral background noise, which is sometimes joined by a chorus of croaking toads and frogs. Huge fruit bats flit around in the early evening before they finally settle, hanging upside-down in the branches of the large trees. These are quite scary as they are about the size of flying squirrels! When it goes dark, tiny little fire-flies dance around in the garden which is quite a magical sight to see. There are also tiny weaverbirds around here which are fascinating to watch when they are building their nests. They fly into the palm trees, take hold of a long palm leaf in their beaks and then fly off, stripping a long portion of the leaf as they fly away. They then weave these raffia strips intricately, in and out and round and round, repeating the process until an incredibly beautiful little round ball has been formed, which is suspended from the very end of a slender branch of a tree by what looks like the merest thread. Just a tiny hole is left for the exit and entrance of the small bird. When I first saw these birds I thought they were an exotic tropical species with extremely long tails, not realising that they were actually trailing a long frond of palm leaf behind them.

Lizards are everywhere. At first I was really startled by their appearance but they are harmless and people say they get so used to them that they hardly notice them any more. The males are quite large with bright red heads and green bodies, while the females are a plain dull brown colour by comparison. They are amazing creatures and look quite pre-historic. They scuttle around very quickly, stopping to bob their heads up and down as if homing-in on some radar beam, then if they smell danger, shoot off in the opposite direction at a fast rate of knots. Sometimes if they are caught, by a dog or a bird or trapped in a corner, they can apparently shed their tails and often escape with their lives by doing so. The tails grow again, so no harm is done! The little white geckos are also very fascinating to watch. These live mainly in the house and are wonderful at catching insects at night as they run up and down the interior walls. They are quite translucent, so you can see the dark insects inside them if they have had a particularly good night on patrol! Their four feet have little sucker pads on the soles, which enable them to stick to the walls and ceilings. I drew the curtains one morning, and one dropped on my head, which made me shriek with fright until I discovered what it was. That little fellow lost his tail with fright too that morning, but at least he lives to tell the tale!

In addition to the steward and gardener, we also have a night watchman called David. He sits on the veranda all night on a piece of cardboard! He doesn't speak very good English and it is very hard to understand him. They all speak a degree of 'Pidgin English,' which gives rise to much hilarity from time to time. It is taking me quite a while to learn the meanings of some of the words and expressions but the children have picked it up very quickly, and now, cheekily, use it when talking to each other on occasions.

During the very first week I was here I wanted to try and explain to Francis our steward, what we wanted for lunch that day and I couldn't find him in the house. I went into the garden and as Israel was there I asked him. "Where is Francis?'

"Gone for shit Madam' came back the innocent reply! There was no answer to that so I retired quickly back into the house until my embarrassment and shock had subsided. The next word I learnt to my cost was the word 'chop.' In Pidgin English, this means 'eat.' In my innocence, while explaining to Francis how to cook cottage pie, I said, 'First you chop the onion before you fry it with the meat.' This confused him terribly because he thought he had to eat the onion before he prepared the rest of the dish! You can imagine the laughter all the expatriate couples have together when recounting mistakes they have made. One couple told us of the time when some people they knew were having an important dinner party to entertain visiting company bosses who were out from UK. They had pulled out all the stops to try and prepare a magnificent spread from the paltry choice that was available in the shops. The lady of the house said to her steward, when issuing last minute instructions before serving up the feast, "Joshua, before you bring in the pig's head on the plate, please will you place a tomato in the mouth and some lettuce leaves in the ears?' When the lady rang her little bell, the steward

37

duly appeared proudly bearing the pig's head on a platter, but with the tomato and lettuce leaves stuffed into his own mouth and ears!　　Another story recounted was when an expatriate wife was giving a dinner party and was tired of her steward trying to bring all the dishes in and out of the kitchen to the table, banging the kitchen door as he came backwards and forwards.　"Emmanuel, why don't you use the hatch?' she said at last in despair.　"Ah yes Madam I will' came the reply.　Next time 'Madam' called Emmanuel from the kitchen to clear away the dishes, he dutifully clambered through the hatch! Of course!

*　　Must close now, as Brian and the children will be home for lunch soon. They all leave so early for the office and school so I have quite a long morning to fill but at least they are back for lunch which is good.*

*　The airline still haven't found our missing case yet but I'm going down to Lagos tomorrow with a couple of the Pfizer wives, so hope to be able to get some new clothes for Nicky.　He's having to wear borrowed clothes at the moment poor little chap.*

*　　Haven't received any letters from any of you yet.　Hope all are well.*

*　　Love to all the family, from all of us.*

As Always,

Maureen xxx

Brian's boss and colleagues at Pfizer had all been so very helpful and friendly. It was a tradition among all the companies that when a new family arrived from the UK, the company wives did all they could to help settle the new people in. It was after all a totally new experience and indeed I was very lucky to have the help and friendship of all the expatriate wives in Pfizer. They were lovely people and we have all stayed lifelong friends. The friends we made throughout our sixteen years in Nigeria really took the place of our families. We relied on each other so much for everything. Support, help and a shoulder to cry on were much needed in those early days. It was after all a hardship post and many young families who came out just couldn't stomach it and very quickly returned home. Those that did stay had to enter into the spirit of the country in order to survive. It was a unique experience; one that we wouldn't have missed for anything. We had so much laughter and also many tears along the way. At times when we were there, we hated it and yet when we were away on our annual leave, we looked forward to going back. Somehow the sights, sounds and even the smell of Africa got under our skin.

My first visit to Lagos was an education in itself. Our case still hadn't turned up on the Thursday after our arrival. Nick was the worst affected as all of his clothes were in that case except the ones he arrived in. A mistake in packing that I was never to repeat, I might add! Nick had to have his undies and shirt and shorts whipped off him and rinsed out while we were at the pool every day. We did manage to borrow some clothes for him from other people by the following Monday morning but I thought a trip to the shops in Lagos would solve all our problems! How wrong I was!

Two of the Pfizer wives were in the habit of going down to Lagos shopping one day a week, in a company car with a driver. They invited me to join them on the Thursday after we had arrived. They had large cold boxes in the boot of the car, and I soon discovered why! The road from Ikeja to Lagos is called the Ikorodu road and was reputed to be one of the most dangerous road in the world.

CHAPTER 3 - CULTURE SHOCK

Livestock Feeds Ltd
PMB 1097
IKEJA
Lagos State

Sept. 22nd 1970

Dearest All
*   Just thought I would tell you of my first trip*
into Lagos which was quite an experience! I'm still not
sure I have recovered yet! Carole, who is the wife of a
colleague of Brian's, arrived at our house with
Marjorie, another Pfizer wife, who only just arrived
in Nigeria a short time before us, and a Nigerian
driver who worked for Marjorie's husband.
We set off from the quiet orderliness of the GRA at
about 8-30am and turned onto the Ikorodu Road
shortly after. We ran into total chaos straight away.
Buses, Mammy wagons, taxis and cars, all full of
Nigerians, seemed to be competing as to who could get

to Lagos in the fastest time! Dodging all of this traffic were literally hundreds of people, taking their lives into their own hands, hell-bent on crossing the road at any point they wished to. There was simply no order anywhere. No zebra crossings, no traffic lights, not even a central barrier to control the chaos. The road is wide enough but doesn't have 'lanes' and consequently cars and buses overtake on either side of you at will. It was terrifying.

All the way down on both sides of the road, are a complete mixture of old and new buildings. There are houses and shops, offices and workshops, huts, market stalls, and bus stations; in fact a huge, sprawling metropolis for the whole of the fourteen miles or so into Lagos. Everywhere was so busy and congested it was impossible to take it all in. As we approached one of the large bridges that connects Lagos over the lagoon, the most overpowering and awful smell I have ever experienced came in and 'hit' us through the open car windows. This was from the' night soil' that is tipped into the Lagoon daily, having been collected from the streets of Lagos by a truck with a huge 'bin' on the back. The drivers of these vehicles always wear swathes of cloth which completely cover their heads and faces. You would understand why if you experienced it! Carole, a gorgeous girl who is about five months pregnant, warned me about the smell in advance and got out some tissues, which she quickly sprayed with perfume from her bag, and handed them round. I suppose it was better than the awful smell outside, but at that hour of the morning the mixture of the two wasn't very alluring either! Thankfully, I managed to stop myself from 'throwing up' and tried to concentrate on the sights instead!

Just over the bridge I saw one hut that had a notice outside written in large crude letters inviting you to 'Call in here for your Coffin!' Propped up alongside the open door were a quite extraordinary array of 'Coffins' carved and decorated in the most amazing shapes and colours. One was a giant replica of a corn cob which was all bright and glistening yellow in the sun! Imagine being buried in one like that. The Vicar would have a fit!

The barber's shops are quite fascinating too. They are advertised by a crudely hand-painted poster on a board by the roadside, illustrating a series of about twelve or fourteen hairstyles. There are no salons as such, so all the work is done outside. The hairdresser sits on a stool behind the customer, dividing her hair into small sections which is then bound with black twine from root to tip. They then continue to weave or build the most amazing styles with all the bound sections of hair. Some are very elaborate 'coronets' while others are tied back or doubled back on themselves individually. This procedure apparently takes several hours to accomplish and the ladies obviously don't unravel their hair until the next visit to the barber which could be several weeks hence. The men have more simple styles of course, usually just cut very short but the funny thing is that their styles are made by cutting a parting right

43

down to the scalp or sometimes the hair is sculptured into shapes, which of course remain until their next visit.   Nicholas said on our second day here, 'We'd better not stay here too long Mummy, or we might grow roots like the Nigerians do in their hair!'   We soon found out that the Nigerians are fascinated by our children's hair too.   They love to touch Sally's long blonde hair.   I suppose the silky texture is quite different from what they are used to. The funny thing is that I set my hair on big rollers to make it curl and the young fashionable Nigerians are beginning to straighten theirs with newly manufactured lotions and potions which is like a perm in reverse I suppose. Likewise, we enjoy going out to the beaches or pools to get a tan, whereas the Nigerians stay in the shade and use new skin-lightening creams to bleach their complexions.

Anyway, I digress, back to the trip. There are several large stores in Lagos and the driver dropped us off outside the Kingsway store first.   Immediately we got out of the car, we were besieged by beggars of all shapes and sizes.   Some were blind, most were deformed in some way, usually with only one leg and a ghastly 'stump' of the other leg, on view, leaning on a crudely carved crutch.   Some even had only a trunk and no legs at all and were either propped up against a post or being pushed along on a sort of wooden trolley by a child or some other beggar.   Others waved and shouted at us to try and catch our attention, or tried to crawl towards us with hands and feet that were either crippled with leprosy or just reduced to stumps, all of them wanting cash, none of them able to work for a living.   I suddenly realised how sheltered I have been all my life from death, disease or anything remotely to do with poverty as dire as this.   I was totally shattered and distressed by the sight.   I was already so hot and tense after the terrifying drive to Lagos, and then having to face up to this, plus trying to negotiate the deep, foul-smelling storm drains that lie, filled with thick green putrid slime, on either side of the road was almost more than I could take in one morning.

It was a tremendous relief finally to enter the air-conditioned interior of the shop.   The contents of the store though, were disappointing to say the least. They displayed scarcely more than the one in Ikeja had, just more of the same on each shelf.   There were a few clothes on counters, but sadly, nothing suitable for Nick.   We went on to Leventis, another store further down the Marina.   This had a few more things and I managed at last to get one shirt for Nick but nothing else.   The meat looked a bit more palatable here so I bought some fillet of beef.   This was a whole fillet but was long, thin and stringy, covered with a membrane of what looked like skin.   The other girls were getting some also and the man behind the counter offered to take the 'skin' off for us. By the time he had done this there was precious little meat left.   My friends put my purchases in their cold boxes along with their own. They would not have got back home again without going 'off' in that heat. A cold box, I discovered, is the most essential item to carry around in the car with you *in Nigeria. We carried on with our shopping expedition, going into UTC and one or two larger stores and then to CFAO Maloney's, which is a French store, where apparently, you can sometimes pick up different items depending on what has been imported recently. It is impossible to write a shopping list here, as invariably you will be disappointed. Carole said that everyone becomes fairly adept at compromise, though it is always a struggle to find an alternative ingredient to get for a dinner party when you have already planned the menu and can only get a few of the items. I am also finding that I suddenly have desperate cravings for things that normally I wouldn't even think about at home. In one store, we saw tomato ketchup and salad cream on the shelves, I started to put several bottles in my basket, only to find that people were grabbing them from me as soon as I put them in my trolley. It nearly caused a riot. I don't really like tomato ketchup or salad cream but I really desperately wanted them then!*

After returning home and relating my first experience of the Ikorodu Road to Brian, he told me of his first journey on it when he had arrived. He had been invited by Bob and Carole, on his first Sunday in Nigeria to go to the large Federal Palace Hotel across on Victoria Island. It has a very nice swimming pool and restaurant and made a change from hanging around in Ikeja where there was very little to do. They had just got about half-way to Lagos when they saw a man who was very obviously dead lying on the side of the road. This was shocking enough in itself but even more so when they were driving back some six hours later to find that the body was still there, though some-one had at least tried to cover it with a large leaf from a banana tree. Apparently if anyone had tried to move the body they would have been held responsible for the burial of the corpse, so everybody leaves it alone until a relative can be found. They do say that 'Life is cheap' here. There is so much death and disease, which is probably why the Nigerians have so many children because the survival rate is not very high. Terrible thought.

On the way back I noticed there was also a wild-looking 'bush man,' as they are known here, who inhabits the centre of the road at the junction where we turned from the GRA on to the Ikorodu road. These people are normally uneducated, homeless vagrants who have nothing and no one to care for them. This poor man had long tangled hair and lived on the scraps that people occasionally threw to him. He lives in the middle of the busy road, surrounded by plastic bags which presumably contain his few possessions. He was completely naked and obviously very mentally disturbed. Perhaps he was high on drugs because he seemed very agitated and risked being run-over while he shouted and jigged around, gesturing at all the traffic that was passing. The driver had to go slowly trying to avoid him and said that sometimes, the man just lay sprawled on the road in a heavy stupor. What an existence!

Well, I must close as we are going out to dinner tonight. We have no televisions here you know so everybody has to make their own entertainment. We do have a radio but it is very frustrating because the minute we manage to get the BBC overseas service, we always get terrible sound distortion and it seems as if it is being done on purpose when the news is on! Brian manages to pick up a newspaper every now and then. I think they come off the airlines if they are spare and are sold at a shop on the way to Brian's office. Sometimes, if we are lucky, we can pick one up from the Country Club on a Sunday morning, but as you can imagine, we don't have much idea what is going on in the rest of the world!

At the end of September, there is to be a public holiday to celebrate 10 years of independence in Nigeria. Brian is planning a few days' 'break' for us all 'up country' somewhere. Will tell you all about it in my next letter if we go.

Hope you and all the family are keeping fit and well. Longing to hear from you.

Haven't had a letter from any of you yet. Hope you have received mine at least?

We are all missing you and send our fondest love to you all.

As Always

Maureen.xxx

We soon became friends with a huge number of people in Ikeja. The many business companies in Ikeja all employed expatriate management whether it was British, German, Dutch, French, Lebanese Indian or Chinese. Consequently, all the clubs and societies had a huge mix of nationalities where one could meet people from all walks of life. As I have mentioned before, there was no television to watch and so after the men returned from work at about six o' clock at night, getting together with friends was the order of the day. Dinner parties were the norm. We either had friends around to dinner ourselves, or went to other friends on most nights of the week. Those evenings when we didn't, we usually retired thankfully to bed in the air-conditioning to catch up on much-needed sleep. We usually played cards, dice or darts after dinner and generally had a lot of laughs.

Our house had a very large compound so we had a badminton court laid out which was floodlit and also a table-tennis table and so spent many happy hours having a game or two with friends before dinner in the evenings. We also held many 'Sports Days' at our house, when we invited friends and their children, usually at a weekend when there was no golf competition for the men. We organised knock-out matches throughout the day for the adults with badminton, table-tennis, darts and putting competitions, and with games for the children such as hula-hoops, races in the compound and all sorts of other things to keep them occupied during the day, usually ending up with a big barbecue supper for everyone.

There was a large Guinness Brewery on the Industrial Estate near the Pfizer office, and Brian, together with some of his Pfizer colleagues, were invited to join the Guinness expatriate staff there after work on Saturday mornings in the bar and enjoy a bevy or two of the local brew. The Guinness they brewed in Nigeria was apparently stronger than its Irish counterpart because the poorer Nigerians could only afford one drink at a time, and they wanted to feel as if they had had a good drink for their money. They also brewed a strong Lager called Harp. Heineken was another strong Lager that was brewed out there by the Dutch and was very popular. Coca-Cola, Fanta Orange, Sprite and 7-Up was also manufactured in Nigeria and everybody bought those by the crateful.

I had never been in the habit of buying fizzy drinks before, but the water was not safe to drink from the tap and we had to boil and filter every drop before using it. Our water was actually delivered from Pfizer on a big truck, which was then piped into the tank at our house. There was always a huge shortage and so we had to take care that none was ever wasted. Sometimes when it was really bad, we used the same water over and over again, from the bath, which we all had to share, before washing the clothes, and then to washing the floors, which were done daily, before finally using it for the toilets.

The humidity was so bad that sometimes we had to change clothes three or four times a day. Obviously if you played tennis or sport in the mornings as I did, then I changed when I got home. Sometimes I had to change at lunchtime again and of course we always showered and dressed for dinner every evening, sometimes only able to use two buckets of water for the purpose.   In the early days it was the fashion for the girls to wear long dresses in the evenings. Mainly, it was for comfort and mosquitoes didn't so easily bite your legs if you had on a long skirt. In later years it was quite acceptable to go out to friends for supper in light trousers but never if you were entertaining visiting personnel.   On several occasions when we had some entertaining to do, I used to do the preparations in the afternoons as the steward always went off for a break and it was easier for me to fiddle around on my own. It was really the worst possible time as it was so hot and we had no air-conditioning in the kitchen in the early days.   I remember being quite shocked the first time I felt the perspiration running down my legs and having to go to the bathroom to towel myself off before I could resume.   It might sound luxurious having stewards and gardeners but to be honest, it was almost impossible for us to work in a kitchen or garden in that heat and humidity.   The stewards and gardeners used to get up with the dawn and do all the washing and cleaning while the air was relatively cool.

CHAPTER 4 - VISIT TO KAINJI DAM

On the 1st October 1970 Nigeria celebrated 10 years of independent rule. It was still in the hands of the Military Rulers and General Yakubu Gowan was the President at that time.   He granted a five-day holiday for everybody in the country.   We decided to drive North to a place called Kainji, where a huge Dam had recently been completed, built with the aid of loans from the World Bank, the IMF and other Government loans, and which incidentally, are still being repaid some 40 years later.   In addition to the Hydro Electric dam which is the longest in the world, there was reputedly, a small game reserve and lodge with swimming pool, tennis courts and a few holes of golf, which had all been built by the Canadian engineers who had lived there while they were helping to construct the Dam. It had now been turned into a place where tourists and visitors to the Dam could stay.   It all sounded fun so two other families and ourselves decided to drive up in convoy for a few days' break during the national holiday.

Livestock Feeds Ltd.
PMB 1097
Ikeja
Lagos State
Nigeria

Oct.5th. 1970

Dearest All

Hope all are well.   We were so pleased to receive a letter from you at last and to hear all the news from home.   Everything is good with us and we are all getting used to being here.   In fact, we are finding it all to be quite excitingly different to what we have ever been used to at home.

Sally was quite poorly though a couple of weeks ago. We thought she had just caught a bad cold but in fact ended up with a very high temperature and fever which meant we had to call a Doctor in to see her. It turned out that she had Malaria. We have all been taking our anti-malarial tablets daily since we arrived so didn't think it could be Malaria, however, the Doctor told us that we should have started taking the tablets at least two or three weeks before we flew out to Nigeria in order to build up some resistance before we arrived. Nobody told us that, and Sally must have had a bite from an infected mosquito. We have all been bitten since we arrived so we have to be very

53

careful from now on to cover ourselves with a repellant every day and make sure the bedrooms are sprayed with 'Flit' after the steward closes the windows every evening. She is absolutely fine now and back at school so you mustn't worry about us.

General Gowan declared a five day holiday in Nigeria last week, to celebrate 10 years of independence in Nigeria. Carole and Bob and another couple Peter and Elizabeth with their two girls and ourselves, all decided to go 'up country' for a trip to Kainji Dam for a few days. It was quite exciting for us to go somewhere new! We set off in convoy at 6-15am, calling on the journey at a village we had heard of where leather pouffes are made and embroidered by young boys, calabashes are carved for ornaments and tribal drums are made. The village is called Oyo. It was quite fascinating to watch the men and boys at work. My first attempts at bargaining for the goods were rather feeble I'm afraid. I was told by Elizabeth that normally, you ask the price of the thing you want to buy, then offer a third of the asking price. Gradually, after much good-natured haggling, you should end up paying just about half of what they asked for in the first place. If you can get it for less than that, then so much the better. I'm afraid I wasn't really bold enough, and of course, the minute they see you hesitate, you are 'done for'! We did make several purchases however, and are quite pleased with our first Nigerian-made goods. We bought a small tribal drum with an embroidered leather strap, a couple of small carved calabashes and a set of colourfully embroidered leather pouffes, for which I now have to find something to stuff them with!

It was a long, hot journey and we were finally very glad to arrive at the lodge that evening. The bedrooms were quite sparse, but clean at least and we had an en-suite shower and loo to ourselves. The next day we had a tour round the dam and the buildings that housed the huge Turbine generators that provided the power from all that water for the electricity of Nigeria. There were several other families from Ikeja who were also visiting for the weekend and we met quite a lively contingent of expatriates from Dunlop, who also have a company out here in Ikeja. That evening we all ended up at the Kaderiko Club, which was part of the lodge complex, built by the Canadians who built the dam, and where we were staying. The children were in bed of course, but the night ended up with several people going for a rather inebriated dip in the pool at midnight!

The next morning, we had arranged to go off early before breakfast with Bob and Carole to visit the game Park. Brian, suffering a sore head, didn't make it so the children and I went with them and a driver. We drove for mile after mile without seeing anything other than trees and bush land. The so-called game park did not seem to have any game save for one large bird that flew out from a tree across our path and settled in a tree on the other side of the road. It was almost as if it did it 'on request' for the same bird rose from the same tree and flew back to its original perch on the other side of the road when we were on our way back some several hours later. The journey had given us a better idea though, of how the interior of Nigeria looks in the Savannah region and of how clean the small villages are that we had passed along our way, compared with the filth and squalor that is all too evident in the cities.

The village houses in that area are usually round, with mud walls and palm-thatched roofs. They are swept every morning after the goats have been taken out to find grazing, with a sort of besom brush made out of twigs. In the early mornings, you see the Nigerians in the villages, chewing on a sort of twig. We discovered that this is how they clean their teeth. They chew on the stick until it becomes fibrous at the end and then they brush all round their teeth and gums with the softer end leaving their teeth sparkling white. A new 'brush' is used every day.

While we were at Kainji, we experienced our first tropical line-storm which was really exciting. We had been enjoying an afternoon swim at the pool, where curious monkeys had come to visit and much to everyone's amusement, had even tried to pick something out of Nick's tummy button as he sat alongside the pool. Suddenly from nowhere, a strong, hot wind started to blow. Papers and cards and things started blowing off the tables. Elizabeth, who was with us shouted 'Quickly everybody, you've got about two minutes to get everything under cover.' We all grabbed towels, drinks, clothes and everything we could lay our *hands on and ran back to the hotel bar before the lightning struck and the heavens opened with the most torrential downpour of rain that we have ever experienced in our lives. We stood and watched in awe. Thunder crashed around the heavens, sheet lightening lit up the darkness of the sky with blinding light and the rain bounced high off the concrete surrounds of the pool and also hit the water in the pool with intense ferocity. The noise of the rain on the tin roof above us was deafening and the wind continued to blow parasols and various other objects whirling around into the sky. For a while, everyone was buzzing with excitement when almost as suddenly, it all passed over and the wind and rain died down, the lightning faded to sporadic flashes miles away and within a few minutes, the sun returned as the clouds rolled away, leaving everything steaming and still in the wake of the storm.*

We had to return to Ikeja the next day but we had all thoroughly enjoyed our break. We took a different road home and so were able to see more of the country-side and the small villages that we passed along the way. They were all much the same but the roads are all very rough, red rippled laterite, nothing like those back in the UK.

I'm sure you'll be pleased to learn that Brian has arranged for me to have golf lessons with a Nigerian professional who is visiting the Ikeja sports club from the Ikoyi Club in Lagos once a week at the moment. His name is John Brown would you believe, sounds very English! The Ikeja club is only a big field as a matter of fact, with a football cum rugby pitch, a squash court and a few short holes for golf. There is a small club house with a bar and it is a favourite place for the men who play golf to go to every evening after work and play a few holes before it goes dark and then they all sit at a big trestle table outside having a beer afterwards. It is rather like a pitch and putt course as there are only a few holes and they are mostly par three's. They don't have greens here, but 'browns' which are made by using oiled sand! Very odd. I am having to use Brian's clubs at the moment. Anyway, when I manage to hit the ball, I am really loving it! I hear you ask ' How can you possibly miss a stationary ball?' Believe me, I can!

Must close now. Will write again very soon and let you know how I progress.

With lots of love to you all.
From all of us here
As Always.

Maureen.xxx

CHAPTER 5 - FIRST CHRISTMAS

We had learnt that traditionally, in those days, at Christmas, there was a special three-day cruise on one of the ships that used to go from Liverpool to Apapa Docks, near Lagos. These merchant vessels, the MV Apapa or the MV Oriel, ploughed back and forth throughout the rest of the year, with goods and passengers, taking about a month for the round trip. Many of the expatriates who had done a grueling fourteen or sixteen month 'tour' and had a three month 'leave' due to them, used to find it a wonderful way to relax for ten days on the way back to UK for their vacation. The Christmas cruise was always fully booked as it was a way of eating beautiful food and having a good time being entertained on board a ship. It only sailed for a short distance, just across the equator and back, but was always very popular. We didn't have any holiday due to us in that first year, as we hadn't been there long enough.

Two of our friends from Dunlop had booked to go on it and suggested that if my family could get to Liverpool with a parcel addressed to them, and marked 'to be left on board the ship,' they would collect it for us and bring it to us when they disembarked. My wonderful mother duly packed up a huge box of 'goodies' and drove to Liverpool with it, found out where she had to take it and gave the relevant instructions to many people before leaving it with some trepidation that it would ever get 'on board' a ship let alone to us! Fortunately, it worked, and the joy on the morning it arrived was fantastic. There were toys for the children, presents for Brian and I and wonder of wonders, bottles of tomato ketchup, and salad cream!

There were a couple of night clubs in Lagos, that quickly became great favourites with us. One was called The Bagatelle and the other The Domo. If we wanted to go a bit further afield there was another popular one on Ikoyi Island called The Bacchus. They were mostly run and staffed by Lebanese people who cooked wonderful food and played all the latest pop-music. We don't quite know how they managed to get all these lovely ingredients, and neither did we question it, as long as we could go there for good food and dancing and some fun. And go we did. Often!

Brian frequently went away 'on tour' as it was known, travelling around the Livestock Feed Mills in various parts of the country. He usually flew from place to place, as the roads were not good, and the distances too far to make it feasible. During the Biafran War, the roads and rail links in the East had taken a heavy toll and some of the bridges over the

River Niger which had been bombed had not yet been re-built. Some of the smaller air ports were still having problems as the runways had been destroyed and not repaired. Brian was flying into Port Harcourt one morning and the F27 plane he was on was just on it's final descent when the pilot noticed a cow was casually trotting up the runway towards the plane. Thankfully, he aborted his landing and circled around a few more times until the cow had run off into the 'bush!' On another flight that Brian took to one of the remote airports in the early days, the plane had to land on a nearby road as the runway was in such a bad state of repair.

He also had a close-call on another occasion when in a small Twin Otter plane, which he and a colleague had chartered to take them to the North on business one day, and as they were turning at the end of the runway in order to prepare for take-off, one of the struts which connected the wing to the body of the plane collapsed, causing it to tip over on one side. Thankfully, it happened before the pilot had got any speed up otherwise it could have been a very different story. These sort of incidents were not written about in my letters home, as I didn't want to worry our parents any more than was necessary!

The Eastern part of Nigeria had been badly damaged during the war and in 1970, they had not yet even started any sort of repair or re-building programme, as sporadic fighting was still going on in some of the more remote parts. On one of Brian's first trips there, he and a colleague went to the Aba

Country Club one evening after work thinking they could get a beer, only to find it had been abandoned during the war and was now totally derelict, the small golf course was overgrown and there was even a dead cow floating in the swimming pool!

Livestock Feeds Ltd
PMB 1097
Ikeja
Lagos State

Jan 1971

Dearest All
Our first Christmas in Nigeria! I can't tell you how much we missed you all. It felt really strange to wake up on Christmas morning to find heat and bright sunshine outside instead of snow. Quite unlike all our previous Christmases when we used to huddle round the tree in dressing gowns, opening presents, preparing stuffing for the turkey, peeling vegetables, etc. I'm afraid there was none of that here!
There is very little to buy from the shops here yet, so I'm afraid the children had a rather lean time with their presents on Christmas morning this year!

Books seem to be the only worthwhile thing available to buy at the moment, but I did manage to get an artificial tree of sorts. It is made from wire with 'branches' that are bound around with shredded white and silver cellophane paper. It looked a bit pathetic but when I hung some pink baubles on the ends it looked quite festive! I also decorated all round the living room with lots of Casuarina branches and baubles so it wasn't too bad. The children and I spent an afternoon making paper chains and lanterns out of coloured paper and glue which we strung all across the dining end of the room. I think the steward Francis thought we had gone a bit mad!

After Christmas, Drew and Barbara came round with that wonderful box of presents you had sent out on the ship for us, it was absolutely fantastic. It was like Christmas Day all over again. Thank you so much for going to so much trouble and doing that for us. The children were absolutely thrilled with their presents as you can imagine and so were we.

We spent a lovely evening at the Saddle Club on December 23rd, when a Carol service had been arranged. We have recently become members there and really enjoy going up there so that Sally can continue with her riding. The club is situated a little way out of Ikeja in what is referred to as 'bush country.' It is run totally by the expatriate members who live here but the stable boys who look after the horses are all Nigerian. The clubhouse is a round open structure with a thatched roof, inside which is a Bar with simple tables and chairs on the surrounding *veranda.   After parking your car to one side of the stables, you have to walk through a sort of paddock and up a couple of wide steps on to the veranda which surrounds the Bar. It is lovely sometimes to go up there after Brian finishes work in the evenings and sit and have a drink with friends just before the sun goes down. Most expatriate members ride their horses out into the bush after they have finished work for the day.   All the horses are stallions and usually exceedingly lively.   They are not completely trained and many expatriates, who have never really ridden before, ride them hard, for their own exercise and bravado. Of course there isn't a great deal of time left after work before it goes dark either, and it is very dangerous to ride out into the 'bush' in the dark. There are no real paths or roads through the 'bush' and horses can quickly become lame if they catch their feet on a fallen branch or in an unseen hole.   There have been several accidents with people being flung off their horses, having been caught by overhanging branches, even in daylight, as they charge along at great speed. We were rather nervous at first about Sally riding these stallions. We have been fortunate enough however, to meet one girl who is well trained as an equestrian and who has taken Sally riding with her on one of the quieter horses, or even just riding round the paddock when it is more suitable.*

*   Anyway, let me tell you about the evening of the Carol Concert which turned out to be very special. The pathway through the paddock had been lined with*

'lanterns' all the way up to the clubhouse. These had been made by the members from old tins, in each of which, floated a lighted wick in oil, then a large paper bag had been placed over the top of each one. They very effectively lit the pathway through the paddock and all the way from the intense darkness of the bush, right up to the bar in the clubhouse.

When we arrived, the children, who had been rehearsing secretly for a few days, were whisked away from us to the back of the stables while we got ourselves a drink and settled down on the veranda. It was very dark apart from the moon and stars, the lanterns and a few lights from the bar. After everyone had arrived we were all asked to be very quiet. The crickets and the whinny of some of the horses were the only sounds to be heard. Then very softly from behind the stables came the gentle voices of the children singing 'Once in Royal David's City.' Slowly up the illuminated pathway, came a small procession of children, each one holding a lighted candle, singing the beautiful Christmas carol. At the start of the second verse, we were all supposed to join in, many did, but I was suddenly struck with a very large lump constricting my throat and with tears swimming in my eyes was too emotional to sing just then. It was totally beautiful. In that place that night, in the open, under the stars, with the stable and the horses so near, for those few minutes, we felt that it was truly the meaning of Christmas.

We were invited to spend Christmas Day with Peter and Elizabeth and their two daughters, who we had been up to Kainji Dam with and who are close neighbours. It felt very strange to be eating turkey on a blisteringly hot day. We had no sprouts or any of the usual vegetables associated with Christmas fare. Nevertheless, we had a feast and were made most welcome by them and their friends. We also played silly party games afterwards followed by a dip in their pool. One game went slightly awry when the men tried to drag another chap across the pool on water skis by attaching a rope to him and running as fast as they could from one end to the other! What a laugh! We went to a pantomime at the Country Club the weekend after Christmas which we all thoroughly enjoyed. It was quite funny for us because most of the people in it were members of the Saddle Club.

We hope you all enjoyed your Christmas. We thought about you such a lot, wondering what you were doing. We wished so much that we could have phoned to talk to you on Christmas Day, but we did make several 'toasts' to all our families back home as you can imagine.

We had some friends of the children round to play one afternoon and thankfully they were fully engaged with some of their toys in the lounge when I noticed what I thought was a piece of black cable draped over the railing on the veranda. I went outside to have a look and suddenly this black 'cable' shot off the railing and into the bushes. It moved so fast and gave me such a shock! It was a snake! I called Israel quickly from his quarters where I think he had been *sleeping, and he came with his machete. He didn't find it that day, but later told us that he had discovered a nest of them in the roof of the garage! I think they were black mambas. One of the deadliest snakes around! He said he had got rid of them. We sincerely hope he has!*

I will write again very soon and many thanks to all the family for the lovely cards and letters we received well in time for Christmas, and for the fantastic presents that we received from you afterwards!

Lots of love, from us all
As Always,

Maureen.xxxx

In the early 1970s, it was the norm in Lagos to dress for dinner every night, the ladies in long dresses, and if you went out to a night-club, the men wore white tuxedo or dinner jackets. If you were going to friends' houses, the ladies usually wore long skirts or dresses, as this helped repel the ever-present and fiercely biting mosquitos, and the men wore smart trousers, shirts and ties. 'Red-sea rig' was usually worn by the men when the dinner was formal but held outside, so they wore tuxedos or dinner jackets but were invited to take off their jackets because of the intense heat and humidity. Those were the days when bright cummerbunds and matching bow ties were all the rage!

The music and dancing was fantastic in the 1970s. Many nights we would dance the night away at either the Bagatelle or the Domo, or if we went further afield, to the Bacchus club on Ikoyi Island. Strobe lights, loud music and laughter, hot steamy bodies gyrating the night away to jazz, jive, rock'n'roll or smooch, we had it all, and it kept us fit and slim! Sometimes we didn't return home until dawn which was all very well on Saturday nights, but during the week, the men had to be in the office by 8am. It didn't seem to put them off though and as we had no TVs in those days, we entertained ourselves nearly every night either with friends at home, or out with friends. We also began to acquire a large collection of records, both LPs or singles for our new stereo player. Music became a huge part of our lives as it entertained us every evening, wherever we were. We even danced in our own homes or our friends' homes most evenings. The equipment became more available in Nigeria during the next few years and we all had record players, and tape decks, where we made our own reel to reel tapes of continuous party music, with huge speakers supporting various tweeters and boosters, enabling us to blast it out at tremendous volume.

Bobby Benson's, or the Cabin Bamboo, as it was otherwise known, was the night club most local to us. This was half-way down the Ikorodu Road in Ebutte Metta and was a popular venue for Nigerians and some expatriates. The music was always live, very loud and mostly 'Highlife.' To watch the Nigerians doing the Highlife was quite amazing. Some swayed slowly from side to side, depending on the rhythm of the piece, others were more energetic, with bottoms thrust out, feet shuffling to the music, they moved, facing their partner, mostly on the spot but sometimes sinking slowly in the rhythm all the way to the ground and back up again. We all became adept at doing it but it was quite taxing on the thigh muscles. The Nigerians could keep it up for hours and it was quite hypnotic when the music was slow.

Many of the up and coming bands from Nigeria started their careers in Bobby Benson's club. Fela Ransome Kuti being one of them. He became a sort of spokesman who, through his music and songs, protested loud and long about the conditions of the Nigerian people, the poverty, and the corruption in Nigeria, particularly during and after the recent Biafran war. The Nigerians were colourful people and the young among them were so eager to bring change to an oppressed nation. We often thought they were trying to run before they could walk. Many of the older generations didn't want the changes that were being wrought. The fact that Military Rule was in force with a new young President, Yakubo Gowan from the Army being in charge of the whole country, didn't please the old tribal Chiefs. This was perhaps understandable because he was not from one of the three major ethnic groups but from a minor Northern tribe.

I remember on one of the occasions when we were at Bobby Benson's late one evening with friends from the saddle club, they used to have a raffle or a Tom bola during the course of the evening and our friends held the winning ticket......the prize was a young goat! It turned out to be a live one of course!   The thought of trying to get it in the car to drive back home in the early hours   quickly made them hand it back to be drawn again!

CHAPTER 6 - THE GOLF CLUB

When we first arrived in Nigeria, Brian had already become a member of the WAAC sports Club in Ikeja. This was the West African Airways Club, and they had a small piece of land in the GRA on which was situated a wooden 'pavilion' containing a bar where you could buy drinks. Inside, was little else other than a large empty room and a veranda where you could sit outside in some shade. There was a field where you could play football or rugby or at times even cricket and there was also, rather surprisingly I thought, a squash court. This was a very basic concrete structure consisting of four walls and a floor but no roof!

The Nigerians were mad on football, and used to play this on the hard baked earth, mostly with no shoes on, as boots and shoes were not readily available to buy at this time, or if they were, not many could afford them after the war. The expatriate members had also put in a few holes for golf in the top field. There were several short holes mostly like a pitch and putt course, some crossing each other in the middle and with just one longish hole which enabled the players to use a wood for the first shot! Brian had played golf in UK for a few years before we went to Nigeria, and was very keen to keep it up, so was very enthusiastic about playing and developing the club there in Ikeja. There was already a well established golf course in Ikoyi Island, Lagos but this was too far to go on weekdays after work and only really possible at the weekends. All the expatriate men who worked at Pfizer were keen golfers, so Ross, the MD, had no problems when it came to membership of the WAAC club. He was one of the first people to be out there playing every weekend. Brian had written in his letters home to me about the golf section and how they used to race up there after work in the evenings and play the few holes before it went dark at around 6-30pm every night. Then they would sit outside the 'clubhouse' at a trestle table, talking and making friends with other expats from various companies who were also keen to play golf. He told me that I must learn to play as soon as I got to Nigeria. My father was an excellent golfer, and had also encouraged my mother to play. My mum gave me an old set of her clubs and when the packers came to collect the few items that we were allowed to send out to Nigeria with us, I remember one guy saying rather sarcastically, when he saw the old golf bag with about 6 old clubs in it, 'You're not taking those things are you?'

Our 'loads' didn't arrive from England for some weeks, so I had to borrow Brian's clubs. I did have a slight idea as to what I should be trying to achieve, as I had caddied for my father when I was young, and watched him on countless occasions as he used to swing a club in our garden or putt on the carpet in our lounge. I had always thought it a bit of a nightmare game when I was young and never thought I would ever want to play. Little did I know just how hooked on the game I was to become. The first few lessons I had were both frustrating and rewarding at the same time, as I am sure everyone who is learning to play golf soon discovers. It is a wonderful feeling when you finally connect but despair and despondency can overwhelm you when sometimes you find you miss the ball completely on many many occasions. How can you miss a ball which isn't even moving? Tennis was still my favourite pastime but I was willing to give golf a 'go.' There weren't too many girls in Ikeja who played golf in those days so it was quite easy for me to go up to the club early in the mornings and hack around, practising without the fear of being laughed at for the many mistakes I made! We didn't have 'greens' in Nigeria of course, because of the climate, so we had 'browns' instead. These were made out of a mixture of old engine oil and sand which usually had the 'hole' somewhere in the middle of the circle. This had to be swept after each group had finished playing the hole, because of all the deep footprints that were left by the players. This was done by an ingenious home-made contraption consisting of a broom handle to which had been attached a hessian sack. You started at the hole and walked round and round from the centre of the brown to the outside, thereby smoothing the sand and wiping away all footprints on the brown, ready for the next players.

73

In those first days, the browns tended to dry out rapidly and were rock hard at times, mainly because we didn't have committees or proper management of the course, just volunteers who wanted to make the facility as good as it could be at the time. Sometimes your ball would bounce so high after hitting the brown that it could end up as far away as it was when you hit it, or if new oil and sand had just been put on, it could stop and sink in as soon as it hit the surface! Once you got the hang of chipping and putting on the browns though, it was usually quite straightforward as there were no 'borrowed lies' or curves in them as there are with greens.

Brian used to play with Ross and two or three other senior management of various companies on Sunday mornings, and they arrived one memorable morning for a competition, to find a Nigerian body hanging by his neck from a tree on the third hole! They decided it would be more respectful to leave that hole out that morning but discovered later that some of the competitors had already just played round him!

Before long, more and more people began to join the club and we had to think about expanding the facility as there just wasn't enough room for more than a few people to be on the course at the same time. It could be quite dangerous too, as I mentioned, one or two of the holes crossed each other which is definitely not a good idea on a golf course. We had quite a few senior Nigerians, primarily from the military services who were becoming interested in the golf side too. We also had a good bunch of expatriates from all sorts of construction companies working in Nigeria, for example, Crittall Hope, Taylor Woodrow, Blackwood Hodge, and various other companies who could be useful in helping to expand the course. The land was quite a large piece that went as far back as the Agege Motor road and the Railway on one side, but we couldn't really tell that because it was thick, unkempt scrub land and trees with no way through. Slowly, slowly the members started to improve the holes, trying to make the odd one longer by digging a bit more land out of the 'bush' and perhaps adding another brown. The senior Nigerians didn't say anything and seemed to relish the fact that the course was being improved, but nobody said who the land belonged to and we all just waited with bated breath to see if it would be noticed.

One day, Duncan, a member and keen golfer, who was a UAC man, working for Greenham Plant Hire in Ikeja at the time, arrived with a huge grader. He flattened a large area of the 'bush' and just carved out another hole for us to use. Nobody objected and nothing was said! Some time later, a chap called Haworth who was also working for another construction company in Ikeja, donated a spare pre-fabricated building for us to use as our clubhouse. Another piece of land was carved out of the bush to enable this to be erected, together with a car park at the side. Again, nothing was said, so the members continued. Gradually, more holes were made and members gave their own time and efforts to keep improving it until we had completed a very creditable 9 hole course.   Some of the members own gardeners planted the grass by hand as it had to be the sort of grass that would grow in the tropical climate. This is the type that runs along the top of the earth and is quite rough as a fairway. It tends to die off in the dry season but as soon as we had any rain, the long seed heads shot up again. Thus we were always allowed to 'prefer our lie' on the fairways. We either left in place, or planted new palm trees or casuarinas to divide holes and of course dug out bunkers in strategic positions to capture wayward drives or pitches to the browns. Committees were formed and it was decided to ask Ross, our Pfizer boss, to be Captain with one of the eminent Nigerian members to be our first Vice Captain.   Sunday Dankaro was a very popular member who was also chairman of the Nigerian Football association. His elder brother John had once played football for the Nigerian team at Wembley stadium back in the 1940s in his bare feet! We also invited Brigadier Mobilaji Johnson who was then the Governor of Lagos State to be a member together with Colonel Diette-Spiff who was then the Governor of the Rivers State. Chief Abioden Sandy was invited to be our president and his brother Shola who was already a member and a keen golfer, was then the chairman of Nigeria Airways. They were all powerful men in the Nigerian community and we began to feel a little more secure!   Brian, together with friends Mike and Bert got together to write the constitution for the club. Bert had been secretary of a large club in UK for many years and had been involved in writing their constitution years before, so he was a very valuable source of information and help. Brian started going round all the big companies in Ikeja to try to raise money for the course and facilities by offering some debentures for membership to the club. Quite a large sum was raised and this enabled us to build a larger terrace, part of which was covered from the fierce sun, and also to build on a small kitchen plus changing rooms for men and ladies. Brian had the honour of being elected Captain twice during the years we were there, and he served on the committee in one position or other for all of the 16 years he was in Nigeria.

More and more wives began to join us and quite soon, we decided to form a ladies'section and try to become affiliated with the LGU. On 21st Jan 1972 I held a meeting at our house to see how many people were interested in the idea and from then on a very keen ladies' section was born. One lady who had recently joined was a very good golfer and had been a member at the Royal Columbo Golf Club. Doreen kept us well informed of all the rules and regulations, the whys and wherefores, and with her guidance we soon found out all there was to know about golf! Together with Doreen and my friend Carole, we wrote to the LGU and set in motion the official start of the Ikeja Golf Club Ladies' section. I had the honour of being voted in as the first Lady Captain in December that year and Rowena was my Vice

Captain. Rowena had started to play golf in Ikeja at around the same time as me.   We were both immensely keen to improve our game by then and started to play together whenever we could.

The clubhouse was formally opened in May 1973 with many officials and Nigerian dignitaries invited to the ceremony. Brigadier Johnson had been invited to cut the tape but couldn't attend in the end. He did, however, send a representative to make the speeches on his behalf. We had a lovely evening with a buffet dinner provided by the ladies, followed by dancing on the terrace.

The golf club became the social centre of our lives.   The men usually met there after work each evening for a sundowner and the women joined them if we had played golf in the afternoon.   It was an unwritten rule that the ladies didn't play at weekends, unless it was a mixed competition, because it was usually the only time that the men could play due to nightfall being around six o'clock every evening. The Ladies held their competitions on a Monday afternoon and as we were such a young club with so many new golfers we hit on the idea of having 'beginners' competitions' and taking a couple of rules every week for discussion and explanation after the prize-giving. As this always took place on the terrace, and many of the men came up in the evenings as well, they all joined in and of course in the process also learned a great deal about the game. The local boys soon found out that a good source of revenue was to be had by becoming a caddie at the golf club. They used to hang around there all day and of course started to play while waiting for a 'bag' to carry. They would use bent sticks or metal piping as a club and some became extremely proficient at hitting the ball a long way. There was also great competition among the caddies as to whose 'master or madame' that they were caddying for was going to win. They were not averse to picking up your ball with their toes and placing it neatly on a convenient tuft nearby without even seeming to look down or shuffle around while doing so! They were also very skilled at removing the individual wrapping from the new balls in your bag and replacing them with really old chopped up balls that they had found or been playing with, and replacing the wrapping so you were not aware until you next came to get a new ball out of your bag that you had been duped! It soon became obvious that we needed a caddie master to keep things under control!

We began to have inter-club matches with Ikoyi, Ebute Metta, Ibadan, and the Blue Elephant, which was a cement factory, built several miles away 'up country' near Abeokuta, by the Blue Circle Cement Company. They had an extensive compound in which they had built bungalows, each with their own garden, for their executive staff. They had included tennis courts and a challenging nine hole golf course, a pool and a clubhouse, which was lovely to go to some weekends for a change of scene. We used to drive up to the Blue Elephant very early in the morning through 'bush country,' arriving while it was still just cool enough to play 9 holes of golf, after which it was usually too hot to play on, and we would slide thankfully into the deliciously cool water of the pool. If it was an organised match we would normally have a typical West African curry lunch and spend the rest of the afternoon dozing under the shade of the trees, swimming or just relaxing until it was time to set off back to Ikeja before dark.   There was also an air-conditioned bar in the clubhouse, which contained a snooker table, so often the men preferred to stay indoors and play snooker or darts, in the close proximity of the bar! During the school holidays the children used to love going there to the pool, as it made a complete change from the Country club near home.

The talents of the members of the Ikeja golf club didn't stop at golf.   Two of our friends got together and wrote a fantastic pantomime one Christmas.   Ian and Colin, who were both very talented writers, re-wrote Peter Pan to suit our cast and it was a resounding success, long remembered by our children and adults alike. All the members pulled together again, making the stage, the costumes, the scenery, and not forgetting the long 'hard' hours put in at the rehearsals, all of which were excruciatingly funny. I was given the part of Tinker-bell and danced around in a tu-tu ringing a tiny bell. Thankfully, I didn't have a speaking part because of course the bell was my 'voice' but it was a 'major' role nonetheless! When it came to the part in the performance where

Tinker-bell is dying and the children are encouraged to shout really loudly to try to get her better again, through all the noise I heard Sally yelling 'Wake up Mum' which brought the house down and I had to stay prone for several more minutes before I could control my laughter and begin to 'come alive' again.

Captain Hook was played spectacularly by Ian and all the cast worked so hard to make it such a success. Everyone, children and adults alike, joined in with all the songs and the jokes, Peter Pan was brilliant, the pirates were hilarious and the consensus at the end was that a very memorable evening was had by all. The pantomime started off with a narrator coming onto the stage and immediately setting the tone of the evening by saying 'Ladles, Jellyspoons and Chilblains, I come before you to stand behind you, and tell you a story I know nothing about!' All the children remembered those opening lines for many years afterwards and indeed they were repeated again the following year, when, due to popular demand Ian and Colin once again pooled their talents and excelled by re-writing the story of 'Snow White and the Seven Dwarves,' specifically for our members, which proved to be equally hilarious and successful. On this occasion I was chosen to play the part of Snow White, with lots of words to learn this time.

All went well however and was again remembered for many years afterwards. I was shopping in Kingsway one day several weeks after the second pantomime when a little girl stopped in her tracks in front of me and then went rushing back to her mother. I was a bit perturbed so when I met them coming towards me down the next aisle, I asked 'What did I do?'

Her mother was laughing as she told me that her little girl had rushed back to tell her that she had just seen Snow White doing her shopping!

We also started having a regular 'film night' at the golf club on a Wednesday evening. One of the members had a contact in Lagos where we could go and pick up a 16 mm film to rent for the night. Sometimes they were really old and badly distorted but other times we were lucky enough to get fairly new ones. 'Love Story' and 'Jaws' were memorable ones of the period and as we had no television in those days, we thoroughly enjoyed the evening's entertainment with our fellow members. We used to erect a huge screen on the terrace in front of the club house and watch the film sitting in the inky blackness of the hot tropical night. The stewards would serve drinks when the reels finished and had to be changed. When the children came out for holidays we tried to get films that were suitable family entertainment so that we could all join in. I remember that we took the children to see a film in the UK once, during a school holiday, when we were 'on leave.' Half way through the film, Nick whispered to Brian, 'Dad, when are they going to change the reel? I'd really like a drink'

CHAPTER 7 - FIRST LEAVE

The first time I went back home on leave was in June 1971, when I flew out to Amsterdam on KLM with the children and stayed overnight before taking a flight to Manchester the following afternoon. Immediately we got on the plane, the children asked for apples to eat as it had been so long since they had had one! Whilst in Amsterdam, we teamed up with Rita, a friend from Ikeja who was also on the same flight, and staying in the same hotel, so together we toured the city the next morning, went for a boat trip on the canals and then to a diamond factory to see how the diamonds were 'cut' and polished.

Once back in the UK, my mission was to try to find a suitable boarding school for Sally to attend in September since she was now ten years old, she was too old to continue at the Grange school in Ikeja and the only alternative in Nigeria was to go down to the American school in Lagos every day. Knowing how bad the traffic was on that terrible Ikorodu road and how many fatal accidents occurred daily, and coupled with the fact that if she had attended the American school, she wouldn't have done the same curriculum needed for university placement in UK, we were left with no alternative other than to send her back to UK to boarding school.   All Sally's friends from the Grange School were due to be going away to new schools in September anyway, and Sally was really looking forward to doing the same.   My parents had sold the family home while we had been away, as it was getting too big for them to cope with on their own, and my sister Jenifer had just had her third son so there was no room for us to stay with them, as my parents were also staying there until their new house was finished, so we went to stay with Brian's sister Dorothy and husband Ron.   I booked many appointments to see various schools before deciding on St. Mary and St. Annes school in Abbots Bromley Staffs.   Brian came back on leave two weeks later and approved our choice.   New school uniform was bought and name tapes stitched on everything and it was all very new and exciting.   Brian returned to Nigeria in August and I stayed on until Sally started at Abbots Bromley at the beginning of September.

I decided I would stay on until she had her first exeat two weeks later just so that I could see her again and be sure she was settling in well.   From her letters, she sounded as if she was really enjoying herself and was making friends very quickly.

Sadly Brian's father died suddenly just nine days after she had started school. Brian returned from Nigeria for the funeral a week later and then Nick and I flew back with him the following week. It proved to be a very sad end to our first leave. We did have the joy of seeing Sally again though before we went back and it was good to see that she was settling in well to her new school and to meet some of her new friends. I remember saying goodbye to her at the entrance to her junior house and just as we had got into the car to drive away, with huge lumps in our throats, she rushed back to the window of the car and said 'Have you got any sweeties? We might be having a midnight feast tonight!' It brought back all the memories of the schoolgirl's books we had read that had romanticised life in a girls' boarding school. I think that overall Sally did enjoy her school days, even though she soon found out that it was not all midnight feasts and pillow fights in the dormitories!

It had been lovely and exciting having our first leave and seeing all our families and old friends again. We didn't have a home of our own in UK any more and so by the time we had moved around and stayed with various friends and family during our leave, we were quite looking forward to going back.

Nigeria never became 'home' to us because we didn't actually own anything out there either, so we joined the rather rootless expatriate population who came and went, some only fleetingly and others, like us, who stayed for many years. We did subsequently buy our own home in Walton on Thames a couple of years later which proved to be a fantastic base for us during our years abroad, especially as it was within easy reach of Heathrow and Gatwick airports. Later on when Sally went to College in London to study languages and secretarial skills and Nick went to Kingston to take Graphic Design, and I went back to college to study Beauty Therapy, it was a lovely home for us all to be based in, and easy for Brian to commute to and from airports, and London.

In 1972 Brian decided that Nick would also have to go to school in the UK. Most of his friends had already gone and the teaching standard at the Grange School was not very good in that period. He had several Indian teachers and was not really learning anything to the standard he should have been achieving. He was beginning to get into mischief with one of Israel's children who lived in the compound. One day Grace, Israel's wife, came to me with a large melon which had been rather smashed and mangled. It appeared the boys had been throwing stones at it! The owner, who was a friend of Grace, was not best pleased and I had to pay her the equivalent of what she would have sold it for in the market! Nick was rather bored and unchallenged at school with most of his friends away, and only looked forward to finishing at lunch time and getting to the pool at the country club.

When next we were on leave in the UK we went to visit Smallwood Manor which was the preparatory school for Denstone College and fairly near to Sally's school in Staffordshire. Nick was very young, only seven years old, when I finally had to take him there in the following September. He was very brave about it but I know that he always hated going back to school. Through the years, it never got any better for us. We missed them both dreadfully and longed for the time when they would be on the plane back to us for the school holidays. Brian was steadfast in his belief that we were doing the very best for the children, and that, hard though it was for all of us to be apart, they would only benefit in the end. The school holidays were of course joyful occasions when all the children returned on the planes that came to be known as 'The Lollipop Specials', and the holidays revolved around activities that we laid on especially for the children. We were reminded several times of one of the speeches that Brigadier Johnson had once made at the golf club, when he remarked with 'tongue in cheek' that he noticed that expatriate families usually arrived on their first 'tour' in Nigeria, with two or more children, several suitcases and a dog. It wasn't long afterwards, he noted, the peculiar habit of the British who then used to send their children back to UK but kept the dog! We all laughed heartily at his little jibe at the time but because of the circumstances in Nigeria, he was right! It was a sad fact but true.

At the Golf club, the ladies section arranged golf competitions in the school holidays, where the children competed in age groups, accompanied by an adult of course. Nick won his age group in the 5-7 year olds and later in the 8-12 year olds, in addition to winning the annual father and son competition. Sally also did equally well and we always felt it was a pity she never took it seriously as she could have become a really good golfer. Along with all the golf club activities, we organised many competitions and activities at the Country Club.   There were many afternoons swimming at the pool, in which Sally excelled, trips to the beaches at the weekends, barbecues, overnight stays with their many friends, parties and games that were non-stop until it was time to return to UK and school again for another term. This was a time I dreaded. The scrum at the airport was always a nightmare.   Hoards of passengers pushing and shoving to get to the front of the queue, shouting and noise, heat and dust, mothers and children crying, fathers putting on a brave face.

Ikeja only had a very small airport at the time, and one was never quite sure that your child would get on the right plane as there were no huge departure boards to tell you which gate to go to, you just had to walk across the tarmac and get on to one of the planes which were parked on the perimeter.   Even adults had been known to miss their planes on occasions, but their misfortune was more likely caused at the end of a tour when certain individuals had been known to celebrate half the night at the thought of going home the next day and arrived at the airport too late for their flight and rather worse for wear! On more than one occasion, I donned Sally's school 'board' and pretended I was one of the children going back to UK and so managed to get into the departure lounge with them and ensure that they and many of their friends got on the right planes. The chaos was such that the Nigerian officials either turned a blind eye, or else they didn't even notice.

CHAPTER 8 - BEACHES

Lagos sprang up on a series of Islands, which later became joined together by several bridges. Lagos itself revolved around the port that had long been the main trading centre for Nigeria. The elite part of Lagos was across one of the bridges which led to Ikoyi Island. In Colonial times, many expatriates had beautiful, large airy homes built along what must have been elegant tree-lined avenues, many with gardens that led down to the waters edge of the creek, enabling them to catch even the smallest breath of breeze in the heat of the day. The ceilings in the rooms were high so a ceiling fan would also create some cooling movement of air and a covered veranda normally ran around the whole house so direct sunlight rarely penetrated into any of the rooms.

There was an established golf course in Ikoyi with an English professional in situ, a tennis and country club and the Ikoyi Hotel which was fairly good by Lagos standards and had a lovely swimming pool in the grounds which was very pleasant to visit for a change.

Another of the islands which was being developed when we were there was Victoria Island. In the latter part of our years there, high-rise blocks of flats were built to accomodate more expatriates and Nigerian executives from the city.

There were several beaches that one could get to from Lagos and some weekends, particularly when the children were on holiday, or if there were no golf competitions, we would go across the lagoon to one of the beaches on the ocean side. Bar beach was the main beach in Lagos. This was a long strip of sand with waves crashing in from the sea and where most of the Nigerians would go. It was also there where the most barbaric executions were carried out. Unbelievably, this became widely known as 'The Bar Beach Show.' From time to time, robbers or criminals would be marched, in chains and shackles, to the beach. There they would be blindfolded and tied to wooden posts that had been knocked into the sand. Usually there were about ten or twelve of them at a time. Then, in front of crowds of hundreds of Nigerians, as it was well advertised in advance in the Lagos newspapers, they would be shot. I think it was supposed to be a warning and a deterrent to others not to break the law, but it seemed to us that it just generated so much excitement among the local population that it almost had the opposite effect. We tended to avoid that beach, and went instead to quieter ones further up the creek.

A visit to Tarkwa Bay was one of our first trips. We went with friends and took cold boxes with plenty of drinks and a pic-nic lunch, setting off early in the morning to drive down to Lagos and go across the lagoon from the Federal Palace Hotel, in a dug-out canoe. These were long and crudely hewn out of wood and even though they usually had a small outboard motor on the back, it was quite normal for them to break down, and then the boys who worked on them had to paddle. This could be quite a hairy experience in a small dug out canoe, especially when huge tankers carrying produce in or out of the port were bearing down on you! We always tried to get across early before it became too hot, as there was hardly a breath of air in the lagoon, and then we had a fair trek on the other side before getting to the lovely bay which was Tarkwa. Several of the larger companies had chalets built on the ocean side. These usually consisted of a fairly basic wooden structure with a thatched palm-leaf roof providing shade. Some of the larger ones even had a small kitchen and if you were lucky, a fridge and calor gas cooker, or a barbecue made out of half an old metal oil barrel. The larger companies such as Guinness and Dunlop even had a toilet in theirs! If we hadn't been invited to a chalet, we had to provide our own shade and so usually we sat in among the many coconut trees that fringed the beach.

It was always amazing to see the young boys who had ferried us across in the canoes, hoist all our loads, i.e. large cold boxes, folding sun-beds, parasols, baskets and all our parafernalia for the day onto their heads, and then set off through the coconut groves and palm trees, almost at a trotting pace, in order to get over the steep ridge that separated the ocean from the lagoon. Once they had got the momentum going, you couldn't stop them, otherwise they wouldn't have managed to get going again!   Other beaches nearby were Atlas, which was similar to Tarkwa but smaller, and Lighthouse beach, which was very large but had an extremely dangerous current and tragically claimed the lives of several expatriates during our time in Nigeria.   It always seemed like fun to body surf in the huge waves that came in to the beach there, but the undertow was so strong and could easily drag you right out beyond the line of the next set of waves, so you just couldn't get back in again.   Needless to say, once we found out about this, we didn't go there very often.

Many of our friends who went to the beach every weekend, built their own small huts, or chalets, further up the creek at a place called Badagari, where the bathing was safer even though the waves were still quite large.   These people were usually members of the Lagos motor boat club who kept their own speed boats there, as there was no other way of getting up this creek other than by private boat. The trip up the creek was quite a long one but the strip over to the ocean side when you got to Badagari was not as far to walk as it was to Tarkwa Bay. Several of our friends from Ikeja had beach huts near Badagari and we were invited to join them for many lazy Sundays, most especially when the children were out on holiday.

Periodically we were invited to spend a night or two at a friend's beach house with several other friends. After speeding across the lagoon and up the creek in a series of little boats, it was really relaxing to get there and set up the barbecue for lunch. The boys chopped fresh coconuts down from the trees, sliced the tops off and poured rum into the liquid inside, making an instant Rum Punch which was truly delicious and very refreshing after the hot journey. We cooked prawns and steaks on the barbecue, swam in the sea or body surfed in the waves if they were large enough. We could lie in the shade of the palm trees after lunch, read books, play bridge, or more energetic beach games, or doze the afternoon away if you felt like it. In the evening, a cooling breeze, gentle as a whisper, blew along the beach and the crabs came out to dance and play along the shore line. It was an amazing sight. Hundreds of crabs appeared and seemed to rise up on two legs and then with large claws held aloft would run into the edge of the water as the waves receded and back up the beach again as the next wave came in, dancing and dodging the foaming water as it ebbed and flowed.

When night fell we only had the moon and the stars, candles and a kerosene lamp to see by. We had to put our folding sun-beds in a square area between four palm trees and then cover the whole area where the beds were with mosquito nets suspended from the trees. The mosquitoes and sand flies came out in force as soon as it was dark.   They always seemed to make a bee-line for me, and I was usually eaten alive during my whole time in Nigeria. I sprayed myself with vast quantities of 'Johnson's Off' repellant before I ever set foot outside, so sleeping on the beach was not a particularly comfortable experience for me, even though it was great fun.   Whenever we went to stay, there was always somebody who had to get up to 'spend a penny' in the night and it was never easy when fumbling around in the dark to even find an exit from the mosquito nets, let alone make sure that they were securely closed again after finding a way back in! Humans couldn't find the way in or out, but the mosquitoes had no problems!   Going back into the sea the next morning was my only source of relief after being badly bitten all night long!

We also had the opportunity to learn to water-ski when we went up the creeks in the speedboats. This was hilarious for some of us, but quite exhausting when you were learning.   I remember it felt as if my arms were being torn out of their sockets until I got the knack of standing up on the skis and then leaning back and keeping my arms straight all the time.   Some of us never got the knack and we had loads of laughs at the antics of some of the guys who were determined not to let go of the tow rope even while they were being dragged along under water with fountains seemingly spouting out of their ears and noses.   All the children seemed to find it very easy to get up and go and had no fear of the speed or of falling in and were soon jumping over the wake behind the boat as if it were second nature.

The beaches that were easily accessible from the mainland were full of traders. They walked constantly, backwards and forwards, along the beaches with all their wares on display; either carried on their heads, their backs, in their arms or however possible. There were wooden carvings, ivory, bronze and brass heads and figures; thorn wood carvings depicting little scenes of Nigerian life, crude paintings, tie-dyed garments, kaftans, smuggled whisky, rum or vodka and English or American cigarettes. They sometimes carried cheese and smoked salmon in a cold box balanced on their heads, or with other food that had been smuggled from the aircraft that regularly flew into Nigeria; all manner of things that we purposely went to the beach especially to buy. You always had to 'haggle' with these traders because they would ask exorbitant prices for their goods. You also had to be very wary of some of the traders who had accomplices with them. While you were haggling with the trader in front of you, the accomplice might be helping himself to the contents of your wallet or handbag that you had left under your parasol behind you. This happened once to friends who were with us when a snake charmer came by and of course we were all sitting mesmerized by the guy in front of us who was blowing a tune on a wooden flute-type instrument to entice the cobra out of the basket. The large cobra lazily reared his head out of the basket and was swaying gently backwards and forwards to the haunting tune, when our friend Francesco, suddenly looked around and saw the snake charmer's accomplice with his hand in the pocket of his shorts, which were hanging in the hut behind us.   Francesco had lived in Nigeria for many years and was well aware of all the tricks the traders got up to.   He shouted loudly and our men all chased him off up the beach, leaving the snake charmer to bat the poor unsuspecting snake back into the basket, snap on a lid and scurry off up the beach away from the wrath of all us women.

Whenever we went to Bar beach on a Sunday we were intrigued at first to see many Nigerians, men, women and children, who were all dressed in long white robes.   These we learned were a religious sect known as the Cherubims and Serafins.   They seemed to conduct their services on the beach behind us, probably in the hope of converting all the people who went to the beach for their leisure, to make better use of their time on Sundays.   They chanted and sang to the music they made with bells and drums. Sometimes we saw them completely submerging their babies into the sea fully clad in their white robes.   We presumed it must have been some form of Baptism for their infants into their religion.

It was always a treat for us when our children were out on holiday, after a hot day at the beach, to go back home and shower before going out to the Mandarin Chinese restaurant in Ikeja for a meal in the evening. We all loved the food they made there and we got to know the proprietor and his family, who also had another company in Ikeja, and they used to 'smuggle' some of the Chinese food they used in the restaurant, inside the crates of goods they imported into Nigeria for their other business. I used to play tennis with the son and his wife and we became good friends. Rosemary, the wife, invited me and three other friends round to her house every week for a while, and gave us lessons on how to cook Chinese food. I also had a Japanese friend who used to come to our house every week for about three months to teach me how to do Japanese flower arrangements, or Ikebana. Her objective was to try to learn how to speak English, as she had very little when she first arrived. She used to wander round our garden and select a few twigs, leaves and about three or five flowers and after rifling through my kitchen cupboards, select a bowl, plate or dish of some sort, and with minimum materials, one pin-holder, and a flat dish, would create a stunning arrangement in next to no time at all.

I also learnt how to play Bridge at around this time. A new class was set up for beginners in Ikeja so I thought I would take the opportunity to learn. It was quite taxing at first as I had never played cards other than 'snap' and 'patience' before. Bridge is an amazing game and although I never became an expert, I spent many happy hours making up a four with friends or playing in regular bridge drives with the girls from the golf club.

CHAPTER 9 - COTONOU

In April 1971, the expatriate families from Pfizer Nigeria decided to drive west, over the border to what was then the country of Dahomey. It had been colonised by France in 1894 and was incorporated into French West Africa in 1904.

Several years of political instability followed and they had no less than six coups between the years 1963 to 1972. Then a Major Mathieu Kerekou from the Army seized power and seventeen years of Marxism-Leninism followed, after which it became known as the Republic of Benin in 1990. The French had established a Fort at Ouidah on the coast long ago in the seventeenth Century, which was used during the time of the flourishing slave trade with the Portuguese and there were also several other trading stations and forts set up along the coast during that time.

Livestock Feeds Ltd.
1097 Ikeja
Lagos State

April 1971

Dearest All
Hope all the family are well. We are fine here. It was lovely to receive your letters last week and catch up on some news from home at last.

We had a public holiday here a couple of weeks ago and so all the Pfizer expats decided to go off and spend a few days along the coast at a town called Cotonou in Dahomey. It is a French West African country and they are mostly French speaking people who live there. Many French expatriates have settled there permanently and have created French patisseries and restaurants which serve beautiful food because they are allowed to fly fresh produce in, on a daily basis, unlike Nigeria. We had to wait for a while at the border while they checked everybody's credentials, and it wasn't very pleasant to see the border guards were all armed with guns but we made it through without any problems and arrived at our Hotel de la Plage just in time for lunch. The hotel is situated right on the beach as it's name suggests. It was quite basic but our room had a balcony overlooking the sea which was great. The surf was fantastic and there was always a lovely breeze on the beach which circulated into our room

99

*making it feel really fresh and quite cool for a change.
The hotel also had a lovely swimming pool with seating
areas all round where we could eat our meals under
the shade of the trees, which all felt very civilised.
Being by the shore of course didn't feel so humid and
everywhere was much more pleasant to walk around.
There were some really good shops in Cotonou, selling
French produce and it made a lovely change to actually
see stuff that we wanted to buy! I bought a bright red
French Fondu set with a cockerel design on it and the
forks to go with it. Can't wait to try it out. There were
even café's on the streets, where you could go and have
a delicious French coffee and croissants or strawberry or
apricot gateaux! Unheard of in Nigeria! The fruit in
the shops was also imported and we were able to buy
apples, real orange oranges and grapes!*

*Sally and Nick had a super time on the beach
playing in the surf or in the pool with the other
children.   There was another hotel nearby called
Hotel du Port where there was a superb disco on the
Saturday night.   We went with another couple and
their son to a very good restaurant at the airport for a
meal that evening before joining the others at the disco
for a short time before bed.*

*The next morning, Sunday, we were up bright and
early as we were going to see the Village on Stilts. This
is in a place called Ganvie, which is situated just north
of Cotonou, built on the Lake Nokoue. Apparently in
the seventeenth   century the two main tribes in Benin
were the Fon and the Tofinu.   The Fons were*

procuring slaves for the Portuguese at that time, in what was becoming a flourishing slave trade which was booming in West Africa. Fearing for their lives, the Tofinu tribe fled to the lake where they thought they would be safe from the Fons if they built their houses on stilts in the water, because the Fon tribe, deemed the lake to be a sacred place and their religious beliefs prevented them from fighting on the lake.

That morning, we were rowed out across the lake in dug out canoes which is the only form of transport, and invited to go into one of the houses that were all built up on stilts above the water. They were quite amazing, all having been built from bamboo with thatches made out of reeds and palm fronds. We had to climb up a very flimsy-looking ladder into the hut. It was quite spacious, being just one huge room where all the family lived together. The little children stared at us from behind the women who were preparing some sort of meal, curious to see these white strangers in their midst. Everything has to be done in the house of course as there is no yard or garden outside. They live on a diet of fish which they catch from the lake and keep alive in a sort of pen in the water just outside their house, which is also made from the reeds and palm fronds, so they are alive in the water until they are ready to eat or sell them. They must trade their fish I suppose for other essential food like maize. The huts were very dry inside in spite of the fact that we could see the water underneath the bamboo flooring. The people didn't speak any English so we didn't learn too much about their way of life which was a pity as I would have loved to learn more. The guide had told us a bit about the history of the place but it would have been more interesting to have chatted to the women. The lake was now a salt-water lake because the French had dug a canal from the sea to the lake for access in around 1855. It was all very fascinating to see how they lived and contended with the difficulties of life on the water.

Sadly, the next day we had to pack up in the morning and we all set off back to Ikeja after a final lunch at the hotel. We smuggled apples and all sorts of goodies like Ricard (a French Pastis drink) mushrooms, cigarettes etc., back through the border by hiding stuff in the spare tyre of the car, and we even tried to burn the bottom of the fondu set by holding lighted matches underneath to make it look as if it was an old cooking pot! It is always quite tense going through the borders here as you never know how the guards are going to react. Normally the offer of a few cigarettes or money is a good ploy, but sometimes, if they are in a bad mood and they find stuff, they will just take everything. We eventually got through OK and arrived home safely. Our steward Francis came out to help us unload the car and as he was carrying the two bottles of Pastis up the steps to the front door, he dropped them! Can you believe it? All our precious booze was gone in one moment! He heard a few choice Anglo Saxon words from Brian that I don't suppose he had ever heard before I can tell you!

Still, we had a really lovely few days' break and all enjoyed ourselves tremendously.   Everything back to normality now and I will write again soon when I get a minute. Hope you and all the family are well and that you are getting some warmer spring weather at the moment.

Lots of love from all of us here.

As always.

Maureen Brian Sally and Nicky. xxxx

After our summer leave in August that year, I remained in England after Brian returned to Nigeria in order to put Nick into boarding school in September at Smallwood Manor, a preparatory school in Staffordshire. He was only seven and a half years old and it nearly broke my heart to leave him there. The Headmaster and his wife seemed to be a very likeable couple who were sympathetic towards the boys who lived abroad.   There were very good facilities with modern classrooms and a swimming pool, all of which were situated in a beautiful parkland estate with magnificent trees and rugby and football pitches for the boys to play in. Smallwood Manor was not too far away from Sally's school, so we hoped that my parents would be able to visit both of them together on their exeat days.   Unfortunately they didn't always tally and so my parents spent many weekends running backwards and forwards to make sure that they were both taken out on their due dates, not to mention double runs to airports when the beginnings and ends of terms didn't correspond either. We could never express enough our deepest gratitude to them and all our family for their constant love and care for our children when undertaking these journeys on our behalf during the difficult years when we were away.

Livestock Feeds Ltd.
PMB 1097
Ikeja
Lagos State

Nov. 17th 1972

My Dear All,
So sorry I haven't been able to write for such an absolute age, but we've had a postal strike here and haven't received any letters, nor have we been able to post any for the last few weeks. I managed to get a couple of letters off to the children from Ghana so I hope they received them. I sent them to Ghana with a colleague of Brian's and he posted them from there.

Anyway, they are petering through again now but I fear that some of the back-log may have been dumped in the lagoon as we have only had recent letters from you and none since just before the strike!

We had a holiday here on Monday and Tuesday, celebrating the feast of Ramadan, so, after the men had played golf all weekend and moreover had another competition to play on the Tuesday, we girls decided to drag the chaps off to the beach on the Monday. We have some friends here who are quite senior in Guinness and it was their turn to have the company chalet on Tarkwa Beach that weekend. They invited us, Veda and Peter and Bob and Carole to join them. Quite a few of the big companies out here have weekend-type chalets on the beaches and company launches to take them across the lagoon instead of having to hang around and take your chance on the 'banana boats', which are just dug-out canoes. It was really marvellous because normally when we go to the beach, we have to sit in the blazing sun and burn, queueing for hours in intense heat, waiting to get to the island or back across the lagoon in the banana boats, feeling sticky and sweaty, full of sand, sunburnt and very uncomfortable. This time, it was so civilised it was hardly true. We sped quickly across the water in the Guinness launch and over to the chalet, which is built of wood with a thatch of palm leaves, and is situated among the coconut trees, thus providing plenty of shade. It has a steward who works there permanently, a kitchen of sorts, two bedrooms, a shower and even a flushing loo! (Though where it flushes to we don't enquire too closely!)   We had a marvellous day surfing on boards in enormous waves, we ate plenty of food which we had taken with us and drank copious quantities of ice cold beer, as there was even a calor gas fridge in the kitchen.

By the time the evening came, the girls decided that it would be fun to stay the night. The men had to return home as they were playing in a golf match the following day in Ikeja, so they went off in the boat leaving us four women and five children remaining on the island for the night.

It was really quite exciting, being left on the island when all the expatriates had gone home. We had no food left apart from a couple of tins of baked beans but we managed to buy some bread, bananas and tins of milk from a local inhabitant.   After feasting on that, we walked down to the beach again for a last stroll before darkness fell at around seven pm. We came across an extraordinary sight.   Hundreds of crabs came out of holes in the sand and rushed down to the sea for a swim.   They are fairly big ones too, not large enough for eating, but big all the same. We had great fun chasing these crabs in and out of the waves. If you corner them, they turn round to 'attack' you, dancing and side-stepping at a fantastic pace.   The kids were trying to catch them in buckets and coco-nut shells and they were really having a great time in spite of being quite scared about getting nipped by the big claws.

Later after the children were in bed, we girls sat talking on the veranda, with only the light from the moon and the stars and a primitive hurricane lamp. The sounds of the tropical night chorus and the waves crashing on the beach below with a gentle breeze blowing in from the sea, all felt very exotic. We had no air-conditioning that night and we slept under mosquito nets on our sun-beds. We put Veda next to the door with an enormous mallet under her bed! I don't think she was very pleased about that I must say but we all had a laugh. We spent a very comfortable night even though we had no other clothes of course as we had only taken bathing costumes and towelling wraps with us! Thankfully we were quite cool.

The following morning we were up with the dawn and asked the steward if he could go out to get some fish for our breakfast from the locals who were by then, fishing all along the beach. It was a lovely sight to see. They have a circular net which they either cast from the beach at the edge of the waves or from the back of one of their dug-out canoes out in the bay. They must hold it in a certain way because when they have swung it gently back and forth a couple of times, they then fling it out as far as possible and it is wonderful to see it open up and form a full circle before it then drops into the sea. The steward got us several of the small fish that were being caught in the nets and he also came back with some fresh eggs and bread for the children. What a memorable feast we had that morning. After breakfast, we surfed all morning again and then in the afternoon, the men arrived back after *their golf match, bringing cold boxes full of food with them which were transported on the heads of small boys all the way along the beach to the chalet. It was a lovely weekend and we really wished that Sally and Nick could have been with us; we miss them so much and they would have loved every minute. We all went home that night, very sunburnt. My knees and tummy were grazed and sore after being flung up on to the beach so many times by the tremendous waves. It really was super though and we thoroughly enjoyed it.*

Thank you again for having the children for half term. I'm sure they will have had a lovely time, as always. How did you think that Nick was faring at school? Do you think he is settling down alright? We don't glean much from his letters as yet. Thankfully, it will soon be on the run down to the Christmas holidays, and as you can imagine we simply can't wait to have them out here with us again.

Will write again soon.

Lots of love to you and all the family,

As Always

Maureen and Brian.xxxx

CHAPTER 10 -

VISIT TO NORTHERN NIGERIA

Livestock Feeds Ltd.
PMB 1097
IKEJA
Lagos State

March 1973

Dearest All
        Hope you and all the family are fit and well.
We are fine here. We've just had a really exciting trip
to the north of Nigeria. It made a super change for
me to get out of Ikeja and explore a really different
part of the country. Brian was due to go on a trip to
the North to promote the sales of Livestock Feeds, to
check up on the Mills in Kaduna and Kano and also
to introduce a new man who has recently come to work
at Pfizer here. Normally, Brian flies up to Kano and
between the other mills in the North to complete his
business but this time, it was planned that they would
drive up and explore a vast amount of business
opportunities along the way by visiting poultry and pig
farms, cattle breeding stations, and other Agricultural

programmes that are being set up by the Government in the north of the country.

The new chap joined Pfizer last August but his wife only arrived in Nigeria in November. Brian thought it might be a good opportunity for Dick and his wife Judy and I to drive up with them and see a whole new part of Nigeria, which is quite unlike Lagos, with all the squalor that we are used to seeing here.

We set off on Monday the 26th Feb. at approximately 9 o'clock in the morning. We had decided to take two cars as you never know what might happen on a long journey up country through the bush. We were suitably loaded with provisions of tinned food and water in case we couldn't get much to eat or drink along the way. The two Peugeot 504s set off in a slight drizzle, which was the first rain we had seen for months, and proved to be a delightfully refreshing start to our journey.

Our route on the first day took us through the university town of Ibadan. It is the most populated town in Nigeria, after Lagos, and thus is similarly squalid and overcrowded. I think I told you once that some members of our Golf club in Ikeja were invited last year, to send a team up to the university campus to play a golf match on their course, which was great fun and we plan to reciprocate every year. It had been a joy on that occasion to drive into the quiet well-ordered, beautifully-planted grounds of the campus, after the chaos, noise and dust which is always prevalent on the streets outside.   This day though, we drove on through the town which was crowded with people, traders, buses, taxis, herds of goats and animals, as usual, and on to Oyo, where Brian and I had stopped at the small workshop we had been to once before on our way to Kainji, to show Dick and Judy a local family at work, carving traditional designs on gourds and calabashes.   It was quite fascinating to watch for a while and of course we had to buy some for our collection.   The gourds are quite delicate to handle and I was skeptical about getting them back home in one piece as we had a long drive ahead.   I'm pleased to say however that they did survive.

On our next stop, while we were having a pic-nic lunch under the shade of some trees by the roadside, we were suddenly startled to find a woman crawling slowly towards us through the long grasses.   She was begging for food and water, and we were horrified to notice that she only had stubs for fingers and toes.   She was a leper.   There are still many lepers here and it is a pitiful sight to see.   We gave her some of our store of food and precious water and she thanked us profusely, by touching her head, her lips and her heart with her stubby hand before she crawled away again, grateful for our help.

After Ilorin, we had to stop at Jebba.   Here the bridge across the River Niger is used for both trains and vehicles.   We had to wait for a train to cross before we could go again and the heat by that time was intense.   Everything seemed to be shimmering in the early afternoon sun, with not a breath of air and absolutely no shade. The train passed ever so slowly across the bridge before we could set off again. We drove on through the long afternoon to Bida and then to Minna where we arrived just after 7pm. and darkness had already fallen.

We found the old 'rest house' and thankfully they had two chalets for us, which were rather archaic, with no electricity and not very clean either but after travelling 500 miles from Lagos to Minna that day we were only too thankful to crawl under the mosquito netting and go to sleep. The next morning we were amused to see that the elderly steward who had greeted us the night before in his native dress, had dug out his old white uniform and red fez and remembering his old Colonial training was looking very smart. He had cleaned the dust off the table and producing an old 'fly-blown' menu, asked us what we would like for breakfast. Grapefruit, bacon and egg, toast etc., was all on the menu so we all said we would have that. 'Ah Master' said the steward 'No grapefruit,' 'OK then,' we said, ' we'll just have the Bacon egg and toast.' 'Master, No bacon' came the reply. 'OK, egg and toast then?' 'No bread Master!' We ended up with just a boiled egg, which he had obviously had to scrounge from some local chickens that were running around, and a cup of tea, but no milk!

Rest houses were built in the days of Empire by the British Government, in most of the main towns in Nigeria. British Personnel from the Government and the large trading companies, such as United

Africa Company, (UAC) and John Holt, used to travel around the country and of course needed a place to stay. There were no hotels in those days, so these simple rest houses are small chalets consisting of a single bedroom and washroom. If you are lucky and they are well used, you might even have electricity, but most of those in the more remote areas do not. I think by now, as travel by air is becoming more accessible, these rest houses are seldom used and even though they are supposed to be maintained and usually staffed by an old steward, they quickly fall into disrepair and hardly ever have food available, hence our precious box of provisions!

The climate and terrain became very different as we travelled further Northwards that day. Lagos, being in the tropical belt, felt rather lush and green by comparison. It is very hot but humid in Lagos which is quite uncomfortable most of the year. We also have a tropical rainy season during the summer months and smaller 'rains' in February if we are lucky. In the North, however, it is incredibly dry and dusty with hardly any trees and mostly scrub land for the cattle to forage. Because it is so dry, it did feel slightly cooler in the evenings and early mornings and air conditioning wasn't quite so necessary at night. As long as you are covered with mosquito netting, we found that it was quite pleasant to sleep with the windows open. It rarely rains in the North however, so obviously water is an even more precious commodity. We noticed that a few watering holes had been set up at intervals along our route and the Fulani herdsmen, who were gathered *there with their goats and cattle, must have found it a welcome relief.*

The Government are setting up experimental pig and poultry farms and some cattle stations around the Northern states to see which breeds will survive and breed effectively. It was interesting to see some breeds at the watering holes that looked rather like Friesian cattle, only smaller. We presumed this was a trial at dairy farming, which has been pretty non-existent in Nigeria so far. The huge Brahmin cattle are only used for meat and fresh milk is usually obtained from goats. We never have cheese at all as you know, unless it is from the smugglers who purloin it from the aircraft that come in from abroad.

Brian and Dick went off to see the pig farm at Minna after breakfast which was part of their business plan and we all set off again for Kano at around midday. The fascinating villages that we passed on the way were built of red mud, which had been baked hard in the sun. The houses were all circular in design with little thatched roofs which go up to a point in the middle. Standing a little apart from the circle of huts, was usually a smaller cluster of grain stores which look for all the world like giant honey pots, each with its own little thatched roof that is sometimes cocked up at a rather comical angle, presumably to let the air in. There were also massive termite nests standing more than ten feet tall, which looked like fairy castles with their turreted and pointed spires reaching up to the skies. They are built by the termites out of the red mud of the region which has been baked hard in the sun. Did I ever tell you about the time when we had once returned home to Ikeja, after a day at the beach, to find zillions of giant soldier ants were running like a stream through our garden and past the whole of the front of our house? They can literally destroy everything in their path. Apparently they had gone through the 'bush' to our neighbour's in the next compound and through their chicken coop, devouring all the chickens that were inside as they pursued their relentless journey. The only way we could disperse them and enter our house was when Israel our gardener poured some paraffin on the trail and threw a match into it. It was horrendous but it stopped the trail and they diverted back into the bush again. Thank goodness they hadn't gone into the house! But I digress, and will continue with our trip to the North.

As we travelled on through Kaduna and Zaria in the North that day, we noticed that the huts became more like houses, still made of baked earth but larger, more sand coloured and square in design. The corners of these houses had strange projections and turrets which we can only think may have been some form of ventilation. We were struck by the amazing designs which had been carved into the walls and some of them were coloured with bright red or blue dyes.

When we reached Kaduna and called into the Pfizer Livestock Feed mill there, the manager mentioned to Brian and Dick about a new hotel that was being built on our way to Kano. It was to be called the Bagoda Lake Hotel. It was getting late as we left Kaduna but we pulled off the road about 25 miles away from Kano just to have a quick look at this hotel and couldn't believe our eyes. After travelling for hundreds of miles with nothing but scrub land and scattered villages as far as the eyes could see, there, in the middle of this desert waste was a real 'oasis!' It was like a mirage. There was a luxury hotel, built to British and American standards, with chalets containing bedrooms with TVs, radios and bathrooms. There was also a magnificent restaurant, a bar, swimming pool, floodlit tennis courts, a lake with an artificial beach, a golf course and even an open air theatre! We were truly amazed. It wasn't officially open but the staff were all there, being trained, and after showing us round, they said we could try it out and stay for dinner. We had really good food, very good service and at reasonable cost. We simply couldn't believe our luck, and were only sorry that we had to leave and go on to Kano where we had booked into the old Central Hotel for the night. It is quite dangerous to be travelling on the roads at night. There are no lights or signposts and the roads themselves are little more than laterite which is always deeply rutted and pot-holed, thanks to little or no maintenance and the massive trucks that career along them at enormous speeds. They are rarely repaired even after the heavy rains. Finally, after some confusion with directions, and a rather scary drive in the dark, we were all extremely relieved to arrive at the hotel at about

10-30pm.   It was such a poor contrast to the new one that we had just had dinner in but we were all so tired after the full day's travelling that we were just glad to be there safely and to have a bed for the night.

We lost our way again whilst trying to find the Veterinary department in Kano the next morning.   It turned out to be a happy misfortune this time, as we ended up in the old city which was a truly fascinating place.   There were very narrow streets, clearly built long before the motor car came into existence, with square flat-topped mud houses pressing in on either side.   It was teeming with people wearing their colourful robes and headdresses, and we could only crawl along through the streets very slowly, inviting much curiosity, whilst following donkeys carrying large bulky loads, and children and goats running everywhere.   We also passed the enormous pyramids which are built out of sacks of groundnuts, containing about 400tons each, and are one of the most prolific crops and staple exports from Nigeria.   We eventually met up with the Pfizer agent in Kano, one Alhaji Bello, who, after initial customary greetings and when business was concluded, agreed to take us all around the vast ancient market.   This turned out to be a truly fantastic experience.   We walked our way through narrow alleyways with stalls on either side, selling everything from leatherwork to potash!

One section dealt with accessories for horses and camels.   The tribes in the North are famous for their beautiful horses and of course they hold the very exciting Durbar from time to time depicting a re-

enactment of the fierce battles of the past. The Emirs of Kano and Sokoto are still descendants of their warrior forbears. There are the nomadic Hausa, Tuareg and Fulani tribes in the North and they still ride their beautiful horses, resplendent in very colourful robes, to the Mosques to pray. The horses are equally magnificent with their beautifully tooled leather saddles and bridles, which are coloured and embellished with stitching and tassels in every hue. Guards surround the Emirs, some of whom carry an enormous parasol of gold cloth to keep the sun off the Emir, while others walk alongside with large fans made out of ostrich feathers, in an effort to keep him cool on the way. These saddles and bridles, for horses and camels, are made and displayed for sale in the market, along with the saddle blankets, which are hand woven from camel hair, and ornately embroidered with silver and gold threads. Girth straps, spurs, stirrups and bits, all were sold here in this section of the market. There were precious stones and jewels of all shapes and sizes, coral, agate, moonstone and amber. There was even a money exchange quarter where we saw Marie Therese Austrian dollar pieces which were bought for their silver content and melted down to make rings and jewellery. CFAO francs were also exchanged here by those traders who were crossing into Chad and Niger. Most of those traders were sub-Sahelian in origin, predominantly Tuareg who are distinguishable by their voluminous dark blue or black robes and head-dress. They ride both horses and camels and are famous for their skills with these animals. When they go across the desert, where it is blisteringly hot by day and bitingly cold by night, they normally take their goods by camel train.

Alhaji Bello was calling out the traditional Northern greeting to all the traders as we passed. He was obviously well known there as they all responded in kind. We carefully skirted around the meat market section as none of us had the stomach to go in there. It was situated by the side of an open sewer and the stench from that and the meat, together with the black cloud of flies that filled the air and assailed our nostrils made us choke and retch. The huge chunks of raw meat were just laid out in piles on the ground so that the blood could run off into the sewer. We hurried on past as quickly as the crowded lanes would allow.

There were stalls selling shrunken monkey heads and various strange objects which we did not dare to question, but are apparently used by medicine men, for Ju-Ju rites. There were wooden carvings in vast quantities; stools, heads, masks, made out of ebony and ivory, bronze heads of chieftains and great warriors of the past. Other stalls were selling gold jewellery, some for stretching necks and ear lobes, and bangles and beads of every metal, colour and design. Clay cooking pots, baskets and all manner of goods were all for sale in this amazing place. There were piles of salt, minerals, grain, flour, and spices from the East; flat round baskets full of tomatoes and chili peppers, green citrus fruits and vegetables such as yams, *cassava and corn meal. It was a feast for the eyes as well as an assault of the senses, an experience not to be missed and one I am sure we will never forget.*

Returning from the market, we passed the place where they made the traditional dark blue Tie and Dye cloths that are worn by the Hausa tribes. This process seemed to me to be the same as it would have been in Biblical times. We looked over a wall on to a dried river bed, or Wadi, below us where many people were toiling on the flat rocks, in the intense heat of the near mid-day sun. There appeared to be deep holes in these rocks which were filled with the dark indigo blue dye. The woven cloths, which are first stitched and tied in a certain way, are then immersed into these holes full of the dye, thus not allowing the dye to penetrate into the design that the stitching has created. After some time, the cloths are pulled out and allowed to dry before the threads are broken and the design exposed. We went to the entrance of a nearby hut where the dry cloths were being taken, and saw four men sitting on the floor, in front of a huge log, upon which they were beating the cloth with immensely heavy clubs, keeping up a rhythm for hours on end. Their faces and bodies were glistening with sweat even though it was quite dark and cool in the hut. We could only imagine that they were for some reason both stretching the cloth and at the same time, imparting the material with a high sheen. Alhaji Bello told us that these lengths of cloth were used as turbans by the Hausas and were highly prized by them and the other tribes along the southern fringes of the Sahara, especially the Tuaregs, as they cost more money, which of course added to their prestige. We bought a length as a memento, but it seemed to us to have been a very long laborious process before each short length of cloth was finished. Sadly, our time in Kano had run out and we had to leave. Maiduguri was some 360 miles away and we had to reach there by nightfall.

From Maiduguri, Brian decided that the proposed trip to Yola and Mambilla would have to be abandoned this time as it would not have left enough time for investigating the cattle situation on the way up to Lake Chad which was a main priority of the trip. Before we set off the next morning, as we were filling up with petrol, which was being pumped into the car by hand, we noticed that there were still roughly hewn wooden carts being pulled by oxen along the road. Such a strange mixture of ancient and modern still prevails up here in the North.

On the two hour drive to the lake we were astounded at the enormous numbers of cattle that were gathered at the numerous water holes along the way. Again, it was just like stepping back in the pages of time to drive along that road. There were camel trains and Arab horsemen riding beautiful stallions, with their colourful robes and headdresses billowing out behind them as they rode at speed. Fulani herdsmen were driving the slow-moving cattle on foot towards the water holes. At each water hole, which we judged to be, on average in this region, about five miles apart, there must have been about a thousand head of cattle. What fantastic meeting-places they seemed to be in all that desert waste. Cows, goats, donkeys, camels and horses, all gathered together, patiently awaiting their turn. We wondered if the herdsmen met every day as they passed from one hole to the next, or whether they searched for pastures new. The cattle were typical of Biblical times too, Brahmin mostly, like oxen, with huge horns and a large hump on top of their necks.

When we reached Baga, which was the nearest point to the massive Lake Chad, bordering four countries, Nigeria, Niger, Chad and Cameroon on our map, the road unexpectedly just petered out into the sand, so we had to stop! We could see a small village a short way off with houses built of cane and thatch which seemed to be typical of this area. People started to crowd round us, as we stood by the cars wondering where to go! Shy, yet curious children gathered round us laughing and pointing nervously. Donkeys were in abundance and flies were swarming around and sticking to us. The heat was intense as it was just after mid-day. Incredibly, Brian saw a policeman in full uniform, standing some way off in the village, so he made his way over to ask him where the road to the Lake was! Originally the lake used to come right up to where the road was, but because of the recent years of drought the lake had shrunk considerably and now it was quite a long way away. We couldn't even see it at this point. The policeman *said it was impossible for us to get there by car, but he would arrange for us to go by tractor if we really wanted to go. We said we did, so he directed us back to the nearest rest house where we could wait in the shade until he had arranged for the tractor to take us to the lake. We waited for a long time but nothing came, so eventually, we went back to find the policeman and asked him if we could walk there. He seemed rather dubious but agreed to walk with us. By this time, he had changed into his best white Agbada and red Fez, no doubt to impress on the rare visit of white people to his village. It was still intensely hot and we seemed to have attracted a crowd of curious people, who were following us, which was all a bit embarrassing. The sand was so hot and dirty and very difficult to walk on and finally we began to wish that we hadn't bothered! Our policeman, seeing our obvious distress, called us into a nearby hut and told us to wait in the shade until he went to see if he could find out more about where the tractor might have got to. The hut was possibly a local drinking house as one or two men sat at bare wooden tables drinking Star Beer. They were obviously quite unused to seeing white people in their village as they couldn't take their eyes off us. None of them spoke any English so they just sat silently watching us. The air was foul in there and the walls, ceiling, tables and chairs were thick with flies. After waiting for another half hour we were greatly relieved to hear the sound of the tractor at last and almost glad to get out into the sunshine again. At first, we were quite amused to find that we would have to hop onto the trailer at the back with about twenty Nigerians who were all going to the lake. The policeman, who had returned with them, directed them all to shuffle up to make some room for us and at first we sat on the side of the trailer. The driver set off at a spanking pace through the village and we had to cling on tightly as he careered perilously along the filthy rutted sand, sending up clouds of black dust and sand all around us. We soon realised that we would be jolted to pieces or else thrown off the back. Judy and I eventually couldn't hold on any longer and sank to the floor of the trailer, not caring any more about the filth, the feet, or the amusement in the eyes of all the watching people around us. So much dust, blackened with dirty exhaust fumes which belched forth above us from the vertical exhaust pipe of the old tractor engine, choking every gasping intake of breath, filling our eyes, our noses and our mouths. It must have taken about twenty minutes to get to the lake but it felt like as many hours. When we finally got there and thankfully climbed down from that terrible trailer ride, far from seeing the cool clear waters of the quiet lake of our imagination, we were again surrounded by thousands of people, noise, donkeys, camels, boats, fishermen, filth and flies. Topping it all was the most abominable smell, from the dried and rotting fish that were laid out on the shore, that you could ever imagine. Our visions of a quiet swim in the cool clear waters of Lake Chad had vanished in a flash and all we could think about was to prevent that tractor from* setting off back without us and leaving us there in the midst of all that dirt and chaos and stench. In a further moment of madness I had said to the policeman when we were back in the village, that I wouldn't mind having a go at riding on a camel! My imagination again telling me it might be quite romantic to ride a camel along the quiet waters of the lakeside. Now, here he was, negotiating with one of the fishermen to take us out on the lake in one of his dug-out canoes, and at the same time arranging for me to ride one of the many angry-sounding camels who were waiting by the lakeside, objecting to being loaded up with the enormous sacks of dried fish, ready for their long journey across the desert. Instantly assessing the situation and realising we could be stuck there for a long time, Brian said we were very sorry, but we had to go back NOW!

Our Policeman was understandably perplexed and disappointed and clearly could not understand these mad English people who had driven so far, put him to so much trouble to get the tractor and trailer, had even set off walking in their eagerness to get to the lake, and then when they eventually got there, only wanted to turn around and go straight back again! The trailer was already being loaded up with sacks of dried fish. There was nothing for it, we decided, we had to get on that trailer or we might be stuck there for evermore! As we climbed back on to these putrid sacks, the flies rose in dark buzzing clouds around us. Judy and I squeezed into a corner on the floor of the trailer, while Brian and Dick once again bravely sat

125

on the side.   Immediately, Nigerian people started clambering over the sides until we thought we might be suffocated in the crush.   I had often wondered what it must be like trying to get onto a Mammy Wagon with a crowd of the locals, now I knew!

The journey back was even worse than the journey to the lake had been.   It was painful, to say the least, sitting on that hard metal floor of the trailer, with all the jolts and bumps reverberating on bottoms and spines. Our legs were already crushed under sacks full of fish, made worse with many people now sitting on top of the sacks.   Brian seemed to be sitting on my left shoulder, my right arm was trapped against the side of the trailer and my head was bent on to my knees. Going back also meant that the wind was in our direction so not only did we get all the dust that was churned up by the wheels from the tractor but also the copious amounts of sand and dust that was now being blown by the wind.   When we finally, mercifully, got back to the car, we looked as if we had been down a coal mine for weeks!   We thanked our kind policeman most graciously of course, rewarded him well for his trouble, and begged a bucket of water so we could at least wash off some of the surface dirt before getting back in our cars and returning to the rest house in Maiduguri and blissfully immersing ourselves completely under a cold shower!

The following day, after Brian and Dick had finished their business at the ministry of Agriculture, we set off for Bauchi.   On the way out of Maiduguri we were totally amazed to see another brand new hotel set back on the hillside. The Lake Chad Hotel. How unbelievable! We had stayed yet again for two nights in an old rest house where we couldn't even get a glass of beer and there, right under our noses was a fabulous luxury hotel, by 1970s standards, which even had a swimming pool! We had a quick snack of chicken sandwiches there, just to prove it was real, and wondered how we could have possibly missed this place! There isn't any TV, radio or newspaper advertising here though, so it's not entirely surprising I suppose.

It was a long drive to Bauchi but the countryside was interesting as we were getting higher into the plateau region and there were plenty of rocky outcrops and even a few trees, which made a refreshing change from all the flat wastes of the desert of the previous two days. We were on our way to see an expatriate colleague of Brian, who worked for the Benue Plateau State Agricultural department, where he is responsible for the development of Beef Cattle breeding stations and processing plants. He is effectively importing bulls with known beef qualities and mating them with the local Brahmin cows in order to improve the overall standard of the breed. He has also set up a large abattoir where the cattle are slaughtered cleanly and humanely, although it is still the tradition of the Muslim tribes here, to slit the throat of the animals they slaughter and allow the blood to drain from the carcass before it is eaten. This fact I discovered to my horror one day early on in our first year in Nigeria, when I had gone to the vegetable store in Ikeja to buy some provisions and looking down, saw I was standing in the blood of a goat that was lying just nearby having recently had its throat cut! When we drove past the new abattoir in Bauchi, I shuddered to see a row of enormous vultures sitting on the top of the roof! We arrived at Harvey's house, to find that he had not yet returned from a conference he was attending in UK. We were fortunate, however, as a friend of his was staying at the house, and offered us accommodation for the night as we couldn't get in at the rest house and it was too far for us to travel on to Jos that night before dark. Brian had stayed with Harvey on previous occasions and he recounted to us over supper that night, of the evening when Harvey had taken him up one of the mighty escarpments of igneous rock nearby because, in Harvey's words, "It's absolutely teeming with bloody Baboons.' On that occasion, however, they only saw a few, but Brian said the evening was magnificent. He recalled, it was just before dusk and the air was very clear and all was still. From their height on the top of these enormous rocks, which were created millions of years ago from smooth solidified bubbles of lava, they could look down onto the vast flat plains below which stretched away to a far range of mountains many miles distant. He could see that there were small isolated communities, each surrounded by tall palisades, which dotted the landscape as far as the eye could see, containing round mud huts topped with thatched roofs. 'Honey pot' grain stores, where they stored the guinea corn, were raised above ground level to protect the grain from termites and other vermin. Goats and other livestock were already housed within each palisade for the night. As they were waiting in the gathering dusk for the baboons to appear and night to fall, fires were being lit outside in every compound where the evening meal was then prepared and cooked. Brian described the way that he remembered in the soft evening light, the thin wisps of white smoke from these fires drifting vertically up to the sky in the silent stillness of the evening. Within minutes darkness fell and all that could be seen were the myriads of twinkling lights, from the fires down below. Memories such as these, in the vast open stillness of an African night, stay with you forever.

We continued on our Northern journey the following day around noon. Our next leg took us to Jos which is situated in the Benue-Plateau State. It is reputed to have a lovely climate as it is high up on the Plateau and vegetables and even roses grow successfully there. The British evidently discovered tin there while it was under colonial rule in the early1900s and this was extensively mined and exported until the 1960s. The British also built a Hill Station which is frequently used by the expatriates for periods of rest and recuperation, or R & Rs, as it is known, for in those early days, the 'tour of duty' was usually for three years at a time and it became essential for their health and well-being that they were allowed short periods of rest in a more temperate climate, out of the heat and humidity of Lagos and the Rivers State.

Brian had stayed at the Hill Station on a previous occasion and had met some elderly ladies who had come out to Jos with their husbands when they were all much younger. Their husbands had worked for the British Government, either in the mining industry or as District Officers, and even though their husbands had died many years previously, these indomitable women had stayed on in Jos, declaring it to be their home now, and the climate and life style was perfectly suited to them and their needs.

During our journey from Bauchi to Jos that afternoon, we kept our eyes peeled for the local 'duck-billed' women who are peculiar to that region. They have straw or increasingly large, saucer-like plugs of wood inserted into their lips from childhood, so that their lips protrude eventually looking like the bill of a duck. No one really could tell us the significance of this act, whether it was considered to be beautiful or for some other reason, but the tradition, thankfully now seems to be dying out. In any event, we didn't see any, neither did we see any 'game' when we were passing through the Yankari Game region, except for a few monkeys, which one can see almost anywhere. We did, however, drive through some of the most attractive countryside that we had seen on the whole trip. A twisty road, with many trees and craggy outcrops of rocks; fertile patches of land under cultivation and well-kept villages with the huts made completely out of thatching. We passed a sign saying 'Leather Technician' in a small village called Naraguta, some 5 miles outside Jos, so we stopped and went inside a small thatched hut to have a look. The smell of the leather curing in the vats was absolutely ghastly, but we were surprised to see that the skins which were stretched out to dry at the back, were in a lovely array of colours that we hadn't seen in Nigeria before. Apart from the smell, the leather felt soft and quite luxurious too. In the same hut, a few men and boys stitched the pouffes, shoes and bags that are normally traded in the markets but these men also said they could make jackets for us if we wanted them. Brian and I were measured up, me for a gilet and Brian for a jacket, from styles we chose, by looking at pictures in an old, much-thumbed, clothing catalogue that they had. We then chose the soft brown leather and haggled the price. They were not expensive but as we were rather skeptical that we would ever see the finished objects, we didn't want to pay too much anyway. Surprisingly, they did actually make the jackets and we collected them a few days later, on our way back to Lagos and they are really super. A bit too warm to wear here but I'm sure will be well-used when we come home on our annual leave.

We arrived in Jos at about 3-30pm in the afternoon that day and went straight up to the Hill Station. This is now being constructed as a Hotel, as the original wooden built Rest House had sadly burnt down a short time ago. The new one is being built in similar fashion and on the same site as the old building but with wood and stone. The gardens, which will be beautiful up here, are also being laid out with the natural rocks of the area and filled with many flowering shrubs and even roses, which we never see in Lagos because of the humidity.   We called at the Plateau Golf Club for drinks later that evening and were made extremely welcome by all the members who are mostly expatriates and I was invited to play golf on the Monday afternoon with three of the Lady members.

The next day was Sunday and after breakfast we went to a small museum nearby and later in the day to a local zoo.   We were very surprised to see a fair selection of animals there, including lions, leopards, chimpanzees, various kinds of deer and a horrible pit which was full of hundreds of writhing snakes.   In the afternoon Brian and I played golf at the Plateau Club. This proved to be a very interesting, if tricky, little course, played over twelve holes, which is full of water hazards, and small ravines.   It made a pleasant change from the flat course that our members are presently carving out of the 'bush' in Ikeja.

Brian and Dick concluded their business by lunch time on Tuesday and so we set off on our final long trip back to Lagos.   We drove from Jos to Zaria and Kaduna, having been advised that this was the best road to take!   In fact, it turned out to be the worst road we had travelled on for the whole trip!   We didn't know it then, but even worse was to come. From Kaduna to Kontagora we were on the A1, supposedly the best road in Nigeria!   It was practically non-existent in places.   It was wide enough, but with a *tarmac strip down the centre which was only big enough to take one car. Enormous trucks thundering along in the opposite direction, expected you to veer off onto the dry red laterite at the sides of the road, which was in places down a drop of about three or four feet and could dangerously tip you right off the road. We could easily see now why so many of these trucks lay as overturned and tangled wrecks, mostly burnt out and just abandoned on the sides of the road. None of the trucks careering towards us dropped their speeds and it was up to whoever held their nerve the longest as to who kept to the centre strip and who tipped over, or had a near miss! It was really terrifying. Once or twice we skidded or slewed right across the road in the soft ridges of sandy laterite that lay in thick drifts for miles on end. Dick had a terrible time following us as we spewed up choking clouds of laterite the whole way along, blocking his vision completely. Whenever he could, he drew alongside us and we travelled side by side for a while so that at least we could both see a little. Then another truck would come hurtling along and we both had to drop to the side of the road in order to survive. By the time we reached Kontagora, it was 8-30pm and we had all had enough. We decided to look for the Rest house and stay the night. When we found it, we weren't so sure. It was in total darkness as there was no power at all. What we could see by the light of a candle was filthy and dilapidated. We went across to look at a chalet that was empty. It was full of dust and didn't look as if it had even been entered for years. Surprisingly enough, the sheets on the beds looked clean, and they felt quite soft and comfortable. Anything was better than that bumpy road! The next rest house was 150 miles away so we didn't really have a choice. Brian had looked in the kitchen and had decided that we definitely would not be eating anything from there as it was completely filthy. We went back to the chalet and dug out the iron rations that we had brought with us in the car. We dined 'royally' that night on tinned meat, baked beans, fresh tomatoes and peppers from Jos and dry biscuits. We had to ration ourselves to one mouthful of water each as that was all we had left between us and it was necessary to keep a little for the following morning. Surprisingly enough, we all slept remarkably well in spite of the incessant beating of jungle drums that went on for most of the night and sounded very close to us in a nearby village.*

We got off to an early start as we couldn't wash or have breakfast. The rest house looked even more dirty by daylight! The worst part of all this was that even though we had travelled so many miles the previous day we were still north of Jos! Our route had taken us west, but seemingly, no further south. The A1 from Kontagora to Mokwa had given out altogether and we had a really grim drive over 86 miles on the roughest terrain so far. Great trenches had appeared in the track, deep enough for the car wheels to disappear into completely, making an extremely uncomfortable ride. Despite an air-conditioned car, we were still covered with red laterite

134

dust and in the boot, our cases were thick with it. We reached Ilorin by lunch-time and the rest house was a little better appointed, though not much cleaner than the last one! Brian and Dick had one last appointment in Ilorin, so Judy and I whiled away the next three hours before we could complete the last stage of our epic journey and arrived home thankfully to a hot bath, and home cooking at around 7-30 pm.

Altogether, we had actually had a superb trip as it is so different in the North than it is in the South. Judy and I were very lucky to have seen so much of the country, as so many expatriate wives only ever see their own area. I'm sure the trip was both useful and informative for Brian and Dick but on future trips to the North, I somehow think they will be going by air!

Well, I must finish this letter now. By the way, we went down to Ikoyi last weekend to watch the Nigerian Open Golf match which was being held at the club there. Quite a few of our young British professionals were playing and we followed Tommy Horton round for two days. He eventually won the Title and I had my photo taken with him afterwards! Will try and send a copy back with the children when they come back after Easter. Can't wait for them to arrive, it won't be long now.

We are going up to the Golf Club in Ibadan for the weekend the day after they get here, to play in a golf match there. The club here in Ikeja are sending a team up, plus their families, and we stay with various members of the club in Ibadan. Should be fun. The children will be looked after by wives who don't play golf and there will be plenty of their friends back from boarding schools who will be going too. There is a swimming pool there and apparently a trip to the zoo in Ibadan is on the cards for them this time!

Will doubtless tell you all about it in my next letter. Until then, Lots of love to you and all the family,

As Always.

Maureen and Brian.xxxx

On May 21st 1973 Brian celebrated his fortieth Birthday. Actually he didn't know that he was going to celebrate it other than for us to go out to dinner with a couple of friends, Veda and Peter. We told him that we had booked to go to Antoine's, a good Lebanese restaurant that he always enjoyed going to on Broad Street in Lagos. Unbeknown to him however, we had secretly arranged a private party to be held for many of our friends at the Bagatelle night club in Lagos. Everyone who was invited was sworn to secrecy and as it happened to fall on a Monday, it wasn't too difficult to keep everything as normal. Brian went up to the golf club after he finished work for a quick few holes before dark as usual.

After they had finished playing he insisted on buying his partners a drink and was quite put out when they all seemed to be in a hurry to get away.

Finally, he said to them, well somebody has to stay and have a drink with me because it's my Birthday. Mike, who had been his partner at golf said that he had to go because his wife had promised him scrambled eggs and nukkie if he came home for an early night for a change! The other two downed a quick beer with Brian and left. On our way down to Lagos in the car later, Veda said rather nonchalantly, 'Have we got time to call in at the Bagatelle?' as Samie, the manager had told her that he had got some new records in that we might like to hear. We were quite early so Peter and I agreed that 'yes that would be a good idea!' whilst trying equally nonchalantly, to sound as if it was not all part of a plan!

The Bagatelle was quite an intimate restaurant and dance floor on the top floor of a building on the Marina. There was a small lift which only held about four people at the most and we often remarked that the place would have been a 'death trap' if ever there was a fire, as fast evacuation of the premises would have been impossible. As you got out of the lift there was, oddly, an old deep sea diver's head gear on a plinth in front of you. I have no idea of the significance of this piece but it must have been extraordinarily heavy for the wearer as it was made out of copper and brass. Maybe it would have been good to put on in the event of a fire, we'll never know! You entered the restaurant through a small door alongside the helmet.

When we entered that evening, all our friends were lined up on either side of the door and from the end of the line, Ian stepped out with a large card under his arm. Imitating the TV personality Eamon Andrews and a popular television series at the time, he walked down towards us as he announced, 'Brian Hanson, this is your life!' It was quite hilarious. He had made a sort of booklet with years 1 to 40 depicting cartoon drawings of various stages in Brian's life. Everyone had signed it and we then had what turned out to be a wonderful evening. Mike presented him with a bright red enamel 'piss-pot' which had been made especially for Brian by the company he managed in Ikeja and was part of the 'John Holt industries'. It had been stamped on the lid in white lettering, " 40 SOME HANDICAP" and then around the base of the pot, "FROM THE IKEJA CROWD" Mike had also arranged that all the guests could park their cars in the John Holt company car park in Lagos so that we wouldn't recognise any of them and therefore give the game away before we got in. Carol, Ian's wife had made a cake for Brian, using Livestock feeds cattle nuts, from which she had painstakingly stuck each little piece on a layer of icing sugar to make them stand on end before covering the whole lot with icing and decorating it with 40 candles to make it look just like a real birthday cake.

When Brian saw that Mike and Rowena were at the party, he quietly went up to Samie and explaining what Mike had said earlier at the golf club, asked if the chef could possibly make a plate full of scrambled eggs to give to Mike. This was duly presented to Mike, much to his annoyance, and great hilarity from the rest of the party, while we were all being served steak. He did get his steak in the end though. Colin's wife, Jan had also made a real cake which was presented to him, fizzing with sparklers, after the lovely dinner and which we were all able to share. After the dinner we carried on dancing to all the latest pop-records until the early hours. It was an unforgettable and fun evening, one of many precious memories that we had at the Bagatelle.

CHAPTER 11 - FAREWELL TO ROSS

Livestock Feeds Ltd.
PMB1097
Ikeja

November 1973

Dearest All.
    Hope everybody at home is fit and well?   We are fine here.
        I've just had an interesting, if somewhat unexpected trip to the Eastern half of Nigeria. Brian's boss, Ross, is leaving Nigeria as he has been posted back to UK, so there are a number of farewell parties organised for him and his wife over the next few weeks which means we shall be busy.   I know Brian will miss working with him as he has been a really nice guy to work with and they were so very kind and helpful to us both in our early days here.   An American chap will be taking his place so it remains to be seen how he will contend with the climate and conditions here.   Anyway, Ross and his wife Inese were going on a farewell tour of all the Livestock feed mills in Nigeria.   The idea was for them to say goodbye, and to introduce their American replacements, Kent and Mary, to all the staff in the various territories.   Brian was to accompany them and

so I drove him to the office early on the morning of their departure to Port Harcourt which was to be their first stop on the tour, and then went home and had a shower and washed my hair.   Then the phone rang, and it was Brian to say I had to get to the airport at once as Kent and Mary couldn't make it after all, so I had to go instead! Without any time to think, I flung some overnight gear into a bag and rushed up to the airport, with hair still wet, only just making it in time to get on the flight!

In Port Harcourt, we were met by Mr Collins-Douglas who is the purchasing manager, and Odile Akponna who is the manager of the Aba Mill. We were driven to Aba which is about an hour's drive away.   Aba was the town that was really in the centre of the Biafran Civil war. There are still many scarred and bombed-out buildings and not much has yet been done to rebuild them since the conflict ended some three years ago. We were given a great reception at the mill and everyone came out to greet us and have a group photo taken by an official photographer, who had been specially hired for the occasion. We had to sit for about half an hour in the boiling sunshine while all the mill workers were arranged around the official party and then we had to wait until he took the photos. The camera was really archaic and stood on a large tripod.   Would you believe the photographer kept disappearing under a black cloth to take the photo and then changing the plates at the back of the camera. It was like something out of the Ark!   By the time he had finished our eyes were streaming because of looking for so long into the bright sunlight and we were also expiring by then in the near mid-morning heat.

Inese and I were then taken by the manager's wives, to see the local market while the men did a tour of the mill. After the market, we were taken to the place where they weave the traditional Akwete Cloth which is local to the region here. It is still woven completely by hand as it obviously must have been done years ago except that now, we were amused to see, they have added one or two old bicycle wheels to the equipment, instead of using the traditional wooden wheels for the spinning machines! It seems to be an extremely long and laborious process which takes about two weeks to weave a two-yard length of cloth. The finished result is a very heavy cotton cloth with the traditional designs woven in with silk threads.

We all met up at the Aba Club later for a curry lunch. We could tell that it had once been a thriving expatriate country club but now, rather like the rest of the area, was sadly neglected. The air conditioning had packed up and there were no ceiling fans working. Perspiration was just running off everybody and it was so hot we thought we would expire. Eating West African curry didn't help either! It is quite difficult trying to make polite conversation with people you have never met before, while trying to stop the perspiration from dripping into your curry from the end of your nose and chin!

During the lunch, a tremendous storm broke, which managed to cool things off a little, much to everyone's relief! It was quite exciting in a way, as the volume of conversation rose considerably while everyone was trying to speak over the crashes and bangs of thunder and the torrential rain that was hammering on the corrugated iron roof overhead.

In the afternoon we were taken around a local poultry farm. It may have been an interesting experience for the men of the party, but by that time, I can't honestly say that I was too enamoured about looking at hundreds of Rhode Island Red chickens running around in a covered shed. We all really needed a bit of a lie down by then. There was no respite though, as that evening, the Aba staff had hired the 'Banqueting suite' of the Presidential hotel in Port Harcourt, where we were staying and where we were to be entertained by them for the 'grand' farewell dinner. The hotel is very spartan but actually I suppose is quite grand by Nigerian standards these days, and had after all just been a war zone. The banqueting suite was just a large room where two long tables had been placed down the centre and we all sat facing each other for the dinner. The cream of Port Harcourt society were there, including the Governor of the Rivers State, General Diette-Spiff and his charming wife. During the meal, there were several speeches from the Nigerian Managers, who were all extolling the virtues of Ross and Inese and how they would be greatly missed. Then came the highest accolade that could be offered to a white man, which was the presentation of the traditional robes of the Rivers State, and was given by the Governor and only bestowed on those people to whom they felt were truly worthy of the honour. These robes consisted for the man, of a bowler hat plus a carved walking stick and a fine woollen tunic, rather Indian or Chinese in appearance but traditionally woven with designs of animal heads. The front fastenings are usually made of gold or silver jewellry. They then have a sort of check skirt which is tied round the waist and slightly gathered at one side. There are no trousers but, thankfully for Ross, shorts are worn underneath the cloth. For the lady, a matching 'cloth,' which consists of two layers of the heavy Akwete cloth like the one we saw being woven in the morning. This is floor length and draped around to make a full skirt, which is then tied and tucked at the waist. A Swiss lace top is usually worn with the skirt, together with a very elaborate head tie of the matching 'family cloth.'

This meant, of course, that Ross was escorted by one or two of the senior men to the toilets to be kitted out, and some of the women escorted Inese to the ladies' toilet to be dressed in hers. I went along with the senior women, one of whom was of course Mrs Diette-Spiff, the Governor's wife. The ladies' toilet was quite luxurious for a change, and consisted of a row of toilets in cubicles in one half of the room, and a row of hand basins with large mirrors in front of them in the other half of the room. Among the guests that night was the official photographer who had also been invited to the dinner in order to take photos of Ross and Inese after they had been dressed in their robes, *and he had brought along a young woman assistant, who happened to be sitting quite near to me at the dinner. It was obvious that she was a village girl with little or no education, unlike the wives of the elite business men who were the other guests. The young girl had also decided that she was going to be in on the' dressing' of Inese, and so had unobtrusively slipped into the ladies' room along with the other invitees. Just as Mrs. Diette-Spiff was putting the finishing touches to the beautiful head tie and we were all admiring it in the mirror in front of the basin where Inese was sitting, this young 'photographer's woman,' hitched up her skirt, sat on one of the basins and started to 'pee' in the basin! Mrs Diette-Spiff and the other women were aghast as you can imagine and told her to get out at once. Poor girl, it really was very funny and I almost felt sorry for her ignorance but amazed that even now there are still people here who don't know the difference between a hand basin and a'loo'!*

The following morning, the men left to go back to Ikeja on the early plane. Inese and I were supposed to be going with them, but Her Excellency Mrs Diette-Spiff had requested that we take tea with her and they had also arranged a trip to the oil refinery for us that morning followed by lunch with Mrs Collins-Douglas. As so much trouble had been taken in arranging it all for us, we felt it would be rude to refuse and so, as the men made their excuses 'due to the pressure of work,' etc. it was decided that Inese and I should stay on and enjoy their kind hospitality and so we were duly booked back on a later plane that evening.

After the men had gone, Inese and I were driven to the refinery by Governor Diette-Spiff's Aide-de-Camp and Mr Collins-Douglas. Half way there, the heavens opened and we were caught in a violent tropical storm with a torrential deluge. Such was its velocity that the car broke down. We were stuck for about an hour in the car, quite helpless, until the rains abated and the ADC managed to hitch a lift with a passing car to the refinery where he then sent another car back to rescue us from the bush! When we finally arrived there, they insisted that we completed our itinerary, so even though we were so behind with our schedule, we were rushed around the refinery and then rushed back to take tea with the Governor's wife. I think she thought that English women only drink tea, no matter what the time of day! Even though we were very late by then, we were hurried off to take lunch with Mrs Collins-Douglas and a host of other people who had all been invited and were waiting to meet us. Not knowing quite what white ladies liked to eat, she had obviously decided to play it safe and made everything she could think of. This she proceeded to serve up, all together on one plate! You should have seen it! We had Nile Perch fish, which is delicious and normally would have been quite enough on its own, but with this we also had prawns, chicken, some other sort of meat, don't ask what, but thankfully it had been disguised with a curry sauce. This was all served up on a bed of rice, roast potatoes, cooked plantain, which is like a big banana, russian salad and snails, which were not the small type of escargots as served in France, but enormous things that had obviously been foraged in the bush and looked, and tasted a bit like a rubber tyre! We were so late by then that we had to race through this meal, which was no easy feat I can assure you, for as Inese pointed out later, 'It looked like something the dog had 'thrown up!' in spite of the fact that our hostess had gone to so much trouble in preparing such a feast for us.

Meanwhile, Mr Collins-Douglas, raced up to the airport in his car, whilst we were still trying to make polite conversation at the same time as trying to eat all that food, so that he could check-in for us. Then we had to say our 'farewells' to everybody without obviously looking as if we were trying to get out fast, but even so, by the time we got to the airport the officials said we were too late and even though the plane hadn't taken off yet, they had sold our seats to someone else!

We were taken back to the hotel by the Aide-de-Camp who had driven us to the airport and though he had tried without success to get the authorities there to let us on the plane, fortunately managed at least to get us a room to share for the night. Inese and I had such a good laugh that night talking about the events of the last two days. The next morning we were up very early again, to make sure we were in plenty of time for our re-booked flight back to Ikeja. Just before we boarded, Mr Collins-Douglas proudly presented us with a huge Nile Perch all gleaming wet and dripping, which he had wrapped in a single layer of newspaper, with the head and tail hanging out at either end. Inese

147

thanked him so graciously and then turned and rushed off leaving him to hand it to me to take on the plane.   We collapsed with laughter on the plane, giggling like two naughty schoolgirls.   I'm ashamed to say, I just stuck that fish under a seat and left it on the plane!   Ross and Brian had no idea what had happened to us of course, but hadn't been unduly worried apparently, because as we had been guests of the Governor and his wife they thought we would have been well looked after.   We had another 'farewell' cocktail party to attend that evening at the Airport Hotel in Ikeja and of course had a great laugh telling everybody all about our escapades.

I'm coming to the end of my Lady Captain's year at the golf club and so last week I organised my day at the club for the Captain's prize.   I was really touched afterwards to find that the girls had all got together and provided food and wine after the match as a surprise for me.   That was really good of them wasn't it? I have enjoyed my year so much, in spite of being the first Lady Captain here.   The girls have all been very supportive and helpful to me and I think it has done a lot for my confidence.   It is on the cards that Brian is to be the next men's Captain too.   I know he is looking forward to that challenge.

Last Tuesday, I organised a farewell Bridge Drive in the morning and then drove down to Ikoyi with Veda, where we had been invited to have lunch with the Lady Captain of the golf club there.   After lunch we played an 18 hole friendly with some of their girls. It was really super and I'm pleased to report that Veda and I played really well.

I'm helping out again this year with the concert that the children give every Christmas across at the Grange school. Tomorrow morning is the dress rehearsal and some of the children are so sweet, especially the little ones. Of course we are still rehearsing madly for our pantomime at the Golf Club too. It really is hilarious and I know Sally and Nick and all the children will love it. Did I tell you I'm playing Tinkerbell? I've been making Christmas decorations all afternoon as I don't know when I'll get the chance again. We are having a party here for 40 people which we are sharing with our friends Mike and Ro, but it is actually being held at our house. It should be quite fun for the children to have the excitement of a party on their first night home. We really can't wait to see them again. Hope you have managed to get most of the things I've asked for to send out with them? Christmas shopping here has been a rather dismal affair again this year I'm afraid.

I really must close now and try to have an early night for a change!

We send our love to you both and all the family

As Always

Maureen xxx

CHAPTER 12 - CHRISTMAS TIMES

We always tried to make Christmas in Nigeria a bit special. To begin with, it was so very different to what we had been used to. Our former Christmas holidays in the north of England were usually cold and often snowy and had always been spent together with our parents, brothers and sisters and their families and the ritual of opening presents on Christmas morning, before preparing the huge traditional lunch. Old friends arriving later in the morning for 'open house' drinks and nibbles, which usually went on well into the afternoon. It was generally late afternoon before the guests went on their merry way and the family could all sit down to enjoy what was usually, by then, well overcooked turkey and vegetables! After the traditional dinner, and the girls had cleared away, we would sit by a fire, watchingTV, or playing with the children's new toys, and games until bedtime. Next day, if the weather was good enough we might go for a long walk over the hills, often in the snow before getting home to finish up the cold turkey with an accompanying buffet of ham, stuffings, bread sauce and salads, etc. We would then have more games or films on TV before bedtime, which was all very traditional, enjoyable and good fun.

Christmas in Nigeria in 1973 however, was quite different and one of the most memorable we had. The children were both at boarding school in UK by then. Sally was 12 years old and Nicholas was 8. We had established a very firm circle of friends who all had children of similar ages at schools all over the UK and we had all been planning for months for their return to Nigeria for the Christmas vacation. Times were very hard in the UK at that time and there was a huge shortage of petrol; the miners were striking and power cuts were the norm. Some companies only allowed their employees to work three days a week, as shops and businesses had to buy generators to keep electricity going for heat and light, and generally the whole country seemed to be in a mess. It was headlined in the newspapers as the 'Winter of Discontent.' We were all very concerned that the children would be able to get out to Nigeria at all. Would the planes be able to get enough fuel to keep flying? Would grandparents be able to pick children up from school and get them to the airports? It was all very worrying. In the end, they all found a way, and we were so grateful and determined that it would be a memorable holiday for us all.

Livestock Feeds Ltd
PMB 1097
Ikeja
Lagos State

January 1974

Dearest All,

A very Happy New Year to everyone!
We hope you all had a wonderful Christmas. We have
had a fabulous time and in truth have squeezed so
much in that I hardly know where to begin!

Thank you so much for all the lovely presents you
sent out for us with the children. We were all
absolutely thrilled with them and Nick has been busy
'hardening off' his cricket bat. (whatever that means!)
Hope you got the hamper we ordered from Fortnum's
in time and that you all enjoyed some of it!

We organised a big party at our house before
Christmas, which we shared with friends and which
turned out to be a really good evening, and then came
the pantomime at the golf club, which we had been
rehearsing for months. It was such a huge success.
Most of the members had played some part in its
execution. Friends of ours, Colin and Ian, both wrote
and produced it and we had an enormous cast who
were all club members. The stage and scenery were
also all built, painted and decorated by club members
and turned out to be really fantastic. The costumes

were all made by hugely talented lady members and were absolutely brilliant considering there is a real dearth of materials in Nigeria, being so soon after the war. Never in our wildest dreams did we anticipate the reaction of the audience. From the very first minute the curtains rose on Peter Pan, it was quite amazing. The children laughed and sang their hearts out, fully involved with every moment and every character on the stage. Some cried at Captain Hook's 'cruel' antics and also when Tinkerbell, played by me, wearing a white 'tu-tu,' drank the poisoned medicine and nearly died. They booed so loud and so long at one point when Captain Hook appeared on the stage that, apart from the noise being heard a quarter of a mile away, we thought we would have to drop the curtains if we wanted to restore order again. We just couldn't get on with the show for at least ten minutes. The slapstick custard pie scene near the end was a riot and all in all it had just about everything in it for the children and not forgetting the adults, who all loved it too. Of course, the children all knew everyone in the cast and Ian, who co-wrote it and played Hook, is a bit like the Pied Piper anyway, in that he always seems to 'collect and entertain' the children round him even in every-day life. They all love him.

We went carol singing on Christmas Eve with a crowd of friends. It was rather strange setting off on a hot tropical night in full evening dress to sing carols at friends' houses instead of being muffled up in coats, scarves and snow boots as we used to in UK! We had many among us with lovely voices and even though the drinks were mounting up, the harmonies kept coming long and loud.   We even stopped off at the Mandarin Chinese Restaurant in Ikeja where there is a large foyer on the ground floor and a staircase going up to the restaurant on the floor above.   The floor and the walls are terrazzo and so the acoustics are superb.   We all stood in the foyer and gave the diners above a superb rendering of 'Deck the halls with boughs of holly,' but because of the amount of goodwill, and alcohol, that we had already consumed by then, it turned out to be 'Ring the bells with balls of holly', after which we all collapsed in hysterical laughter, but we all continued to sing that version wherever we went after that!

Christmas Day was spent with friends for a delicious lunch and was followed by yet another party in the evening.   Boxing day was a curry lunch party with mostly the same crowd of friends but was held at another house and then we went on to a 'quiet supper' with another family in the evening.

A couple of days later, our friends John and Livy gave a fabulous 'Arabian Night' party.   All the guests were asked to go dressed in Arabian dress, all of which was home-made of course, but nevertheless they all turned out to be extremely plausible and fantastically innovative.   John and Livy had decorated their lounge beautifully.   They had put a square of red carpet on the floor with a large circular rush mat in the centre and an enormous candelabra in the centre of that which provided the only light.   All around the matting was a circle of very large floor cushions, behind which they had placed folded mattresses as back rests, over which they had thrown some very colourful striped Sahara blankets. Standing behind the circle, and therefore enclosing it, were large pots containing long palm fronds which reached up to the ceiling, making it look rather like the inside of a Bedouin tent. We all sat around the circle on the floor cushions as the food was served, which was all Arabic, and was really delicious. It was served in several little dishes which we all passed around, while eating the food with our fingers. There were little parcels of spicy meat tied up in vine leaves, liver paté balls, all sorts of bean dishes, cucumber in soured cream, fried cauliflower, and rice dishes, to name but a few. Considering there is so little choice in the shops it was a magnificent spread. Just when we thought it was all finished, out came enormous platters of lemon chicken. We all sat around playing silly games after that as we were far too full to get up and dance.

The next day was a hockey match that our friends had all 'foolishly' said we would play for charity. Several of the men in our crowd are quite regular players, though most of us are golfers or tennis players and haven't played hockey since our school days. The men couldn't raise two teams to play against each other, so the women thought it would be quite a laugh to form a team and challenge them to a match! We have one really good player who had been a county player before she came to Nigeria, but the rest of us haven't played for years. We girls decided that the only chance we had would be if we made it as *funny as possible. We decided to dress up as 'St. Trinian's School' girls, borrowing our children's school uniforms where possible. Our friend Jean Rhodes who has a rather large figure was elected to be our referee. She is such a good sport and looks quite like Margaret Rutherford, the actress who played a part in the film 'The Girls of St Trinian's.' Our plan was that as soon as the whistle went for the 'bully off,' we would de-bag the men and run off down the pitch with the ball! If the men should happen by any remote chance to get the ball, then Jean would blow her whistle and call for a 'time-out.' Furthermore, she was going to bring a cold box full of gin and tonics and every time she called for a 'time-out,' she would dish out the gin and tonics, thereby wasting time. We all had a huge giggle in anticipation of what the men were going to be in for. The men had other ideas, however. The minute the whistle blew, the men were off. Deadly serious, they won the ball and rushed off down the pitch passing the ball expertly from one to the other and fired it straight into the goal mouth, scoring the first goal before we had even moved! We were totally shocked. They were seriously there expecting to play a proper match! All of a sudden, we had to get our act together and start trying to play proper hockey or else we would have been annihilated. Dinah, our county player, was amazing. She flew up and down the pitch, daring to tackle the men for the ball. It was as much as we could do to keep up with her speed, let alone collect her skillful passes and progress further with the ball. The girls suffered many torn and painful muscles plus bruised and bleeding shins that day, not to mention massive defeat! It was fun though and we managed to raise some money for the charity and a great laugh for all the spectators! The gin and tonics, were finally dished out at the end, not before time I might add, to a very hot and dehydrated team.*

We seem to have started a tradition at the golf club by having a 'Crazy Golf' competition on New Year's Day. The Captain and committee arrange all sorts of silly things for the players to do on each hole. For example, we may have to drink a pint of beer (or worse) down in one, before playing one hole, or play certain holes with a tennis ball or putt with a ping-pong ball, etc. Sometimes we have to play a hole or two back to front, i.e. from brown to tee; or chip through a swinging rubber tyre, or maybe just play certain holes with the driver or the putter only. Whatever is arranged, we are only given our written instructions for the whole match on the first tee and it is always hilarious. Another stipulation is that it has to be played in fancy dress, with prizes being awarded for the best ones on the day. On New Year's Eve, about a dozen of us all went down to the Bagatelle nightclub and restaurant in Lagos for a dinner and dance. At the table where we sat, were a selection of lovely hats, made from stiff card which all looked very realistic. Our friend Veda had in front of her place, a beautiful black top hat with a veil attached, rather reminiscent of the topper that used to be worn long ago with a ladies riding habit. During the evening, Brian

157

*bet her £25 that she wouldn't wear it at the crazy golf
competition the next day, while riding a big black
horse!   He should have known better! Veda always
rises to a challenge!   In spite of having a hangover the
size of a house the next morning, and having had an
ice pack on her forehead that had burnt a red patch,
Veda arrived that afternoon for the golf competition on
a magnificent black stallion which she had persuaded
a Nigerian Police officer to let her borrow from the
Police College in Ikeja.   The officer led her, mounted
majestically on this magnificent steed, all the way from
the college along the main road and up the long drive
to the golf club and then continued to bring her, still
mounted on the horse, up the steps and on to the
terrace.   Veda was dressed beautifully in a long black
skirt and silk blouse and of course the topper with the
veil.   It was hilarious. All the more credit to Veda too,
because we found out that she was really terrified of
horses. She told us later, that she had driven up to the
College in the morning, still full of the alcoholic
bravado she had felt from the night before!*

*The Police cadets live and train there, and it is
where all the magnificent stallions are also kept.   She
explained her strange request to the officer in charge,
who, fortunately had a good sense of humour and was
delighted to oblige.   He asked her to accompany him
to the stable block to choose her horse.   She very nearly
chickened out when they got to the stables and all these
horses heads emerged from their stalls, towering above
her.   The officer promised he would choose the*

158

'quietest' horse for her and moreover, that his usual rider would never leave her on her own and would lead her all the time. Of course, she was a wild success and we all had a 'stirrup cup' on the terrace of the club house before we started the golf match, and the proud officer then rode the beautiful horse back to his barracks!

Brian was playing in the match with Veda that day and on one hole where we were only allowed to use one arm, Brian chose to use his left arm. He drove off with a wood, missed the ball completely, but did a fantastic follow-through and in consequence tore all the muscles and ligaments in his left shoulder. Veda won the prize for the best fancy dress of course and not only did Brian injure his shoulder but he also lost his bet!

Along with all the other activities, we organise a children's golf competition every holiday. They are always very popular and proving to be an extremely good starting point for playing the game of golf for many of the children here. We divide them into age groups, 7-9 year olds, 10-12 years, and 13-15year olds. Each child is accompanied by an adult who teaches the rules and etiquette when required, so no cheating is allowed, but we generally try to encourage and make the game as much fun for them as possible. It is proving to be increasingly popular and many of the children are playing really well now.

Nick is doing exceptionally well and we have had some of Mum's old clubs cut down for him and he can really hit the ball a long way now and is brilliant at chipping. The little caddies all want to carry his bag,

159

and they take bets on him to win! He is in with a very good chance to win the 7-9 year old section. Sally is also doing really well and has a lovely style. When she connects with the ball, she can also hit it a mile, but tends to lose patience rather quickly when it doesn't do what she wants it to do.

We have now acquired a baby parrot! He is a West African Grey, and when he came to us, had barely fledged. His feathers were hardly grown, and he certainly didn't yet have the beautiful red tail feathers that he is now growing. We had originally got him for Graham Penfold, a colleague of Brian's in Pfizer. Graham and his wife Pauline, have been posted to Nairobi and had wanted to take a parrot with them. Brian arranged with one of his Mill Managers from Benin, a town in the mid west, to try to get one for him. He duly arrived at our house with three baby parrots in a sack, that had been 'acquired' somehow but we wern't expected to enquire too closely as to how! We had them all for a few days before choosing one. They were all such engaging little characters.

The export of a parrot from Nigeria and the import of same to Nairobi were to prove so complicated and expensive that Graham and Pauline eventually decided not to bother. We had grown so fond of the one we had chosen for them by that time, that we were really delighted to be able to keep him for ourselves. He makes us laugh so much with his antics. He is too small to talk yet and is rather shy and afraid of human contact at the moment. This doesn't please

160

Nick at all who just wants to stroke him all the time. We've had a very large cage made for him and try to let him out of it every day so he can get used to being around humans. The steward doesn't like it, as he says 'he poo-poos all over the place!' We've called him Penfold after Graham of course. The first time he tried to fly he had climbed out from his cage onto the sideboard and plodded along to the end whereupon he bravely launched himself into the air. He has had his wings clipped and so only succeeded in falling off the end and landing in a very undignified heap on the floor amid terribly indignant squawks and protestations. We have had a large hoop and a swing made for his cage and he loves these toys so much. He entertains us constantly by doing somersaults in his hoop and one very clever trick he learned early on was to climb up the side of his cage and then get hold of his swing with his beak, then when he gets onto the swing and finally lets go of the side of the cage, this enables him to swing backwards and forwards several times. He loves to do this and repeats it endlessly. We realised very early just how intelligent he is when we noticed that he always ate his food when we were sitting at the table eating ours! I don't think it will be long before he starts to talk. I sit and talk directly to him at least once a day by just repeating one sentence to him over and over again.

Well, I think that I have just about exhausted all my news now. There has been no bread in the shops all over Christmas, what a crazy country this is. Not as crazy as UK sounds to be at the moment though. I *do so hope you will be able to get enough petrol to get to the airport to pick the children up and then take them on to school. Could hardly believe your account in your last letter of only having power for so few hours each day. It's quite incredible what these unions are doing to the UK with all these strikes, holding the country to ransom as they are at the moment. Poor Mum having to cook on a little camping stove! Sounds almost like here now! Our power goes off almost daily too, but that is normal here and happens all the time.*

I will write again soon to let you know the times of the children's flights home. The holiday is flying past all too quickly as always. Don't like to think that it will soon be over and Sally and Nick will be gone again. Many thanks again to you all for our lovely presents. We do so appreciate how much you do for us.

Lots of love to you all.

As Always

Brian, Maureen, Sally and Nick xxxx

Our friends Colin and Jan also held a big Christmas party one year where they actually removed part of the drinks bar that had been built in their lounge, so that they could get a larger table in, to accomodate all their guests. This was rebuilt of course at a later date! After a lovely meal, Colin switched on a recording he had made of the 'Last Night of the Proms' where all the traditional old songs were played, and we all joined in with hearty voices, jumping up to stand and sing at intervals throughout the meal.   As mentioned earlier, we have many friends with beautiful singing voices, who had been primed in advance and   sang numbers of their own choice during the evening.   Having had such a lovely meal and plenty of alcohol, I remember we all became extremely patriotic that night, with many toasts drunk throughout the evening to various friends, families, absent friends, etc, etc.   We finished off a wonderful evening all joining in with enthusiastic renderings of Jerusalem, Land of Hope and Glory and Auld Lang Syne.

   We knew that Graham would be visiting us on business again before long and we decided that the first thing we would try to teach the parrot to say was 'Piss off Penfold.' We were amazed at how quickly he picked it up.   The next thing we taught him was 'Where's Sally? Gone to school!' and then 'Give us a kiss!' Again, after constant repeats of these sentences, he was soon chatting away.   We had been told never to whistle to him, otherwise he would only whistle back and not learn to talk.   When there were people in the room, he generally kept very quiet at first, with his head cocked to one side just listening to all the chattering that was going on.   We used to play lots of darts matches within our crowd of friends, usually after a dinner.   We had a trophy of a 'golden dart,' which we played for regularly and the couple who won it had to do the next dinner and darts evening! Penfold, the parrot, was very popular with our friends too and we used to have to put him outside on the veranda as his cage was in the way of our dart board. We noticed that he started to talk more and more when he thought he couldn't be seen. I played bridge several times a week and often when it was held at our house, we put his cage outside on the veranda or the balcony which was just outside the lounge.

Our friend Jean, our 'hockey referee,' was an excellent bridge player; she was also a very heavy smoker and had a pretty nasty 'smoker's cough.' Penfold soon picked this cough out and started to imitate her in such a realistic manner we often thought it was Jean! Whenever he imitated her cough thereafter, we used to say to him 'Oh dear oh dear, fetch the doctor.' It wasn't long before he had picked up on the whole routine and we were all highly amused when one time, during the quiet concentration of the morning's bridge, Jean coughed and Penfold, from his cage on the veranda said as clear as a bell, 'oh dear oh dear, fetch the doctor!' He became a brilliant talker and among his repertoire, he could blow a very loud 'raspberry' and then follow it up by saying 'More tea vicar?' in a very refined manner! He also used to exclaim 'Oh what a gay day!'and years later when we had our beautiful Giant Schnauzer bitch 'Tessa,' we came back from leave one year to hear the parrot saying in a very authoritative tone, 'Sit down Tessa, damn dog!' We could only assume he had imitated our then steward Ruben, who had been looking after her while we were away. Schnauzers were traditionally bred as cattle dogs and herding is instinctive with them.   Ruben sometimes wore flip flops, and Tessa used to chase after him and nip at his heels whenever he wore them in the house. We presumed that was how he admonished her when she had done that!

    We also had some beautiful guinea fowl that we kept in the compound.   They had been given to us live and were intended for us to eat.   They were so lovely though, that we kept them as pets!   Tessa used to round them up when she was only a very young puppy, and of course Penfold soon imitated their calls too and thought he was a guinea fowl!   We had a long corridor and floors of terrazzo in our house and Penfold quickly imitated the sound of my shoes on the floor, and whenever the phone rang and I used to hurry down the corridor from the bedroom, Penfold would pre-empt me and before I reached the phone, he would have made the sound of my heels clicking on the floor, then in a perfect imitation of my voice say 'Hello,' before going into a series of little chattering noises interspersed with my giggles.   It was quite uncanny.   Of course the most memorable moment was when Graham came to stay with us on a business visit from Pfizer Nairobi.   He had apparently gone to the dining room early one morning and as we weren't yet there had just said when passing the parrot's cage,'Good morning Penfold!'   To which, right on cue, the parrot answered, 'Piss off Penfold!'   Brian and I arrived for breakfast a few minutes later to find Graham collapsed in hysterical laughter on the settee!

Penfold, the parrot, became ill one time and we were very worried about him. We didn't really know what the problem was but he seemed to have a cold as his nostrils were moist and he was very lethargic and not eating his food. We knew Psittacosis was a lethal parrot disease and could also affect humans. Pfizer made an antibiotic called Terramycin, so Brian got me some tablets and I used to crush one in a teaspoon and mix it with a little water. I had to then try to get Penfold to drink from this teaspoon and hope he would get enough to make him better. It was a very worrying time as we were all very fond of him. He eventually responded and thankfully after a while made a full recovery. He did meet a very tragic end however, while we were on leave one year. Some very dear friends of ours had offered to look after him for us while we were away. When we returned from UK, we were told that Penfold had unfortunately had his head bitten off by their alsatian dog. Penfold had by this time, become very tame and loved having the top of his head stroked. He used to stick it out of his cage and anyone passing would just stroke the very soft feathers on the top. Indeed, he loved it so much that even if there was nobody in the vicinity to oblige him, he had learnt that if he swung backwards and forwards on his swing and held his head just at a certain angle, it would go through the bars, thereby allowing the bar to gently caress the top of his head! Our dog was used to this performance of course and usually ignored him.   Unfortunately, our friend's dog apparently didn't like it. They weren't at home when it happened though and so we had to accept that what the steward had told them was accurate.   We were all very upset of course, as were our friends.   It was also quite well known though, that the red tail feathers were often used in some of the 'ju-ju' rites which were still being practiced in Nigeria.   We all missed his antics and lively chatter for a long time afterwards. He was nearly 10 years old by this time, which is actually quite young for a West African Grey parrot as they can live to be well over fifty years of age.

Talking of 'ju-ju' rites, we had a night watchman called David when we first arrived in Nigeria. A couple of years after we had been there, he failed to turn up for work several nights in a row. Brian got someone from the staff at the office to go and find out where he was and to see if he was ill. The man came back to say that David was no longer with us. Apparently, he and another man had both wanted the same woman for a wife.   They couldn't decide between themselves so they went to a 'ju-ju' man (or witch doctor) for advice. The 'doctor' gave them each a potion to drink and assured them that it would decide who would then be the right person to have the woman.   It certainly did decide.   One of the potions contained poison and unfortunately it was our night watchman who was the one to drink it. He died of course, which was very sad, but true.

By this time, we were keeping a few chickens in the compound that Israel, our gardener enjoyed looking after. We all benefited from the fresh eggs and of course, when they had finished laying we also had the odd one for the pot! Israel came to me one day and said that one of the chickens needed to be killed as 'it no go bring de egg.' I said OK, fine. Then he said, 'bring gin!' 'Gin?' I said, 'whatever for?' He explained, 'I go give de gin for de chicken; de chicken, he be happy chicken, happy chicken no be fright so he do give de soft meat when I go kill him!' We always gave him a small gin before he killed a chicken after that but never quite knew if the gin was for Israel or for the chicken! Another amusing example of African logic we heard of through a friend of ours. He told us of the time a friend of his who's wife was in the UK visiting their children, had suspected that his steward had been drinking his precious sherry. He had marked the bottle one night just to make sure and a few days later, noticed that again the level had gone down. He thought 'Right, I'll fix him' so he emptied the sherry into another bottle, which he hid, and then peed into the sherry bottle which he left on the bar. After a few days, he checked again and saw the level had fallen quite considerably. That evening after his steward had served him dinner, he called him back and accused him of stealing his sherry. 'Oh no Master' said the steward. 'The Madam tell me before she go, to no go forget to put de sherry into de Master's soup every night.!'

Livestock Feeds Ltd
PMB1097
Ikeja
Lagos State

Feb. 1975

Dearest All

Haven't heard from you for ages, which is hardly surprising as just about the whole of the country here has gone on strike! I think I told you that the government had given the public sector an enormous pay increase, ostensibly to bring them into line with the private sector, well now of course it means a lot of people who work in the private sector are getting less money than those who are doing menial tasks in the public sector, so they are all going out on strike until they get more money too. There is apparently tremendous communist infiltration at the moment and the unions are all agitating for so much more. They are demanding nine months back pay as well which means that some companies will have to close down. You could get the ridiculous situation, as would be the case with Brian, that his trainee assistant would be earning more than Brian. This all seems to have come about because of the tremendous rise in the cost of living here. It really is getting impossible but what they don't seem to realise is that in order to cover these wage *increases and arrears, everybody will just put their prices up even more and we'll all be in exactly the same boat again this time next year.*

Two of our senior personnel from New York arrived last week on an annual visit and of course the workers from Pfizer here made them their target and staged a demonstration. Brian said it was the funniest sight really. He had been locked in his office at the time but was watching through the window as these two 'big-wigs' arrived and about a hundred workers from the pharmaceutical, plastic and livestock divisions all carrying placards, converged on the car they were in and as they tried to get out they pressed in on them literally pushing these placards under their noses. It could have been nasty, but fortunately it turned out to be quite funny, as half these guys are illiterate and can't spell anyway, so their placards were hilarious. Not so for the Americans though. They made a very hasty retreat back to their hotel where they stayed until they flew back last night! During that little demonstration, it was noted that not a single senior member of the Nigerian staff was in sight. They hadn't been locked in their offices either! It's a peculiar habit they seem to have adopted of locking the expatriates in their offices whenever they want something. Anyway, I'm glad to say that they did let Brian out of his office later! Everyone is still on strike though, the army are on red alert and General Gowan isn't moving out of Lagos. Shops and offices are still closed and the Army has had to step in to restore power and water to the people.

Brian was on the golf course after work the other night when our friend Veda came rushing up saying that their gardener (who happens to be called Hyacinth, by the way!) had gone berserk and was threatening her husband Peter with a machete. Peter had managed to lock himself in the house and Veda had jumped into her car and driven up to the golf course. Brian had just played a shot with his 8 iron on the hole that is right next to the road but immediately, he and his partner, still carrying a golf club each, jumped in her car and went back with her to their house. They quickly overpowered Hyacinth and sent him off with a flea in his ear! He had apparently been demanding an increase in his wage too, thinking if the unions could do it why shouldn't he?

Thankfully, yesterday it rained! First drop we've had for three months. Tempers always get a bit explosive in the dry season so perhaps it will clear the air a bit. This morning we have woken up to clear blue skies and brilliant sunshine and the Harmattan seems to have been washed away with the rain, at long last. It really does seem to have hung around for so long this season.

We decided to go down to the beach again last Sunday, to Bar Beach where they hold the public executions by firing squad. There wasn't one on last Sunday so we had a lovely afternoon. The sea is fantastic there, the tide doesn't go out so the waves pound up to your feet. It is marvellous to bathe in too when the undertow isn't too bad. It can be very

171

dangerous some days. You get wonderful scenes of the fishermen coming home across the bay. They still have these dug-out canoes which are quite long and painted with traditional designs on the outsides. Some carry up to twenty men. It is quite a sight to see about six of these canoes skimming across the bay with one man standing on the back at the tiller. More amazing still to see them turn into a huge wave which brings them crashing up on to the beach at just the right moment. Some of these canoes have now got an outboard motor on the side and the old traditional method seems to be dying out. The old ones have a single sail, usually made from old flour sacks, stuck up on a central pole. They still use the old circular nets to catch the fish though, which they fling out from the boat with huge dexterity and skill. It is quite a picturesque sight. One of them caught what looked like quite a large shark last weekend!

Brian has been asked to stay on here for another 18 months. Part of us doesn't mind, another part thinks it is time to move on. His American boss here, Kent Kheen, has been ill ever since he got back from his Christmas leave. They can't seem to find out what is wrong with him, they have been treating him for malaria but that hasn't worked so are now thinking it must be some form of virus. I don't think he will stay here for very much longer somehow.

I went to the garage to put some petrol in the car the other day. There is such a shortage of everything here now and the queue was miles long.

According to a board which was propped up by the pump, every customer was only allowed so many gallons each and by the time I finally reached the pump, the attendant told me it had finished. I didn't really believe him but when I protested, was told, 'We don't serve whites here.' I was furious but as I was the only expatriate in sight I just had to get back in the car and drive on. That is the first time that anything like that has happened to me. It's getting to be quite unpleasant here at times.

This might amuse you though, I had arranged to play tennis with a friend last Wednesday morning, and thought we had agreed that I would pick her up on my way from taking Brian to the office. I got to her house and knocked on the door, no one answered so I let myself in to the house and shouted out "Hello Rita! Are you upstairs?' There was no reply, so I sat down and waited. Their dog, an Alsation, came round and having sniffed me up and down, settled down at my feet. She was quite a friendly dog I knew, so I wasn't particularly worried. I shouted for Rita again, but still no reply, so I decided to go outside and see if the steward was there. The dog had other ideas however, and when I tried to open the door, she growled rather menacingly at me and showed her teeth! I came back and made a fuss of her again for a while then tried to go to the door again. The dog got there before me and stood in front of me growling again. Finally, I shouted for the steward who eventually heard me, and came across from his quarters. 'Where is Madame?' I asked? "Gone with the Master' was the reply. "Gone

173

where?' I asked.   "She no go tell me, but she was wearing her white knicker and carrying her balls!'

The Nigerians call brassiers 'Knicker for up' and pants, or shorts, 'Knicker for down.'   I suppose it's quite logical when you think about it!   Anyway, he held the dog while I got away from the house and Rita was already waiting for me at the courts.   You can imagine we had quite a laugh about it.

Must close now as I'm giving this to a friend to take home to post in England with her tomorrow. Hope all the family are well.   Can't wait to see the children again, not long now until they are back again for the Easter holidays.

All our love to you all

As always

Maureen and Brian.xxx

CHAPTER 13 - EAST AFRICA

Nairobi, in the Masai language, means The Place of Cool Waters. It stands on a plateau almost 6000ft. above sea level and is about 140 km (87 miles) south of the Equator. It was originally built in around 1899 to be the headquarters of the people who worked for the Kenya/Uganda railway. The British decided to build a railway from Mombasa in the South which had been the old Capital, to Kisumu by Lake Victoria, on the border with Uganda, so that it would open up East Africa and encourage trading by the old Colonialists. Nairobi developed rapidly and became the new Capital of British East Africa in 1907 and eventually the Capital of the new Kenyan Republic in 1963.

The railway cut through the territories of the Masai tribes. They are a proud and noble race of people who still live according to their ancient traditions. Distinctive in their appearance, they are usually very tall and slim and wear a cloth of bright red dyes with many strings of brightly coloured beads adorning their hair, necks, arms and legs. Their hair is usually plastered with a mixture of the red clay earth and animal fat and then tightly plaited or bound in many styles. Some of the men and women wear enormous collars of the brightly coloured beads which they fashion into large plate-like structures around their necks. They also have a characteristic hole in their ear lobes which both the men and women make larger from time to time by fitting in bigger sticks, stones and beads, until they eventually form long loops on both ears. They have a traditional dance where the men jump up from a standing position to prodigious heights. This became a means of them earning money from tourists in the early '70s as the Safari Lodges began to employ several of them to come in to entertain the guests as they were having dinner in the evenings. They are a nomadic tribe generally though and as well as being skilled shepherds are also fine warriors. Their shields are made from animal hides and are also adorned with traditional patterns in colours of white, black and red. Their spears are long and sharp and the young men have to go through a ritual hunting of the lion to display their courage before they become Masai warriors. They live in dwellings called 'manyattas' which are light structures made of earth and dung which they build inside a circle of thorn fencing thus protecting both the men and animals during the night.

The Kikyuyu Tribe are the largest ethnic group of people in E. Africa. Descended from the Bantu immigration from West Africa, they occupied the lands around Mount Kenya. Jomo Kenyatta, the first President of modern Kenya was a Kikyuyu. Like the Masai, their language is mainly Swahili and English. The two main tribes of the areas around Nairobi did not always see eye to eye and there are still many 'clashes' and unrest in the country today.

The Management Centre of Pfizer AFME (Africa and the Middle East) had been situated in Nairobi Kenya because it was deemed to be the best place for the American personnel to live at the time. The climate was wonderful, the houses where the expatriates settled on the outskirts of the city, were large and airy and mostly built of stone. There were shops and offices of 'modern standards', compared to Nigeria and other African countries, and where most of the goods were imported or locally grown. A 'modern airport' in Nairobi provided good connections with America, Europe, the rest of Africa and the Middle East and Pakistan. It also afforded the Americans the chance of going on Safari during their leisure periods. Safaris in those days were not the sort of organised sophisticated tours with rangers and special vehicles that there are today. The early hotels or Lodges as most of them were known, were really quite spartan by comparison. Nevertheless, they appeared to be wonderful to us, and the prospect of visiting them one day had always been my dream.

In the early days of Brian's work in Nigeria, most of the annual budgets, which were the management plans for the next year, were undertaken in Nigeria. Visiting personnel from the management centre Nairobi would descend on us for a week. As the only hotel in our area was not a very good one, the expatriates who worked for Pfizer Nigeria, were usually allotted a visiting guest to house and entertain in the evenings during their visit. The men were tied up with meetings all day and in the evenings we were expected to organise a dinner in our own homes or attend a reception elsewhere with our visitors and some of the staff from the Nigerian office. They were, consequently, quite stressful times for all concerned, particularly as the shops were so short of any decent food or commodities after the war. After a few years it became more usual to hold the budget meetings in Nairobi and so it wasn't until 1975 that I had my first opportunity to go with Brian, as I had been invited to stay with our friends Graham and Pauline, who had been posted to live in Nairobi by that time.

Livestock Feeds Ltd.
PMB.1097
Ikeja
Lagos State

Apr. 10th 1975

Dearest All.
Hope everybody in the family is well. We are fine here.
I think I told you in my last letter that I might be going to Nairobi with Brian when he went for their annual budget meeting in March? We were invited to stay with our friends Graham and Pauline, after the first weekend when the management team and their wives were due to go 'up country' on a pre-budget 'jolly'!
I was so excited to be going. Everything was booked for our flights out on Friday, March 14th. The weekend was going to be spent at the Mount Kenya Safari Lodge, which is owned by the well-known film star, William Holden. Would you believe it, at the very last minute on the Friday of our departure, Brian was unable to come because one of the chaps who works for the Vet Agricultural division had made a complete mess of his budget and Brian was asked to stay behind and help him to work it all

out again. We were all packed and ready to go, and I was so disappointed, so Brian said I should go ahead without him and he would try and make it at a later date. You can imagine that I was really upset that Brian couldn't come with me, but excited that I, at least, could still go. I set off with some trepidation, as I had no idea what to expect on my own. Fortunately I was met by Brian's colleague, Richard at the airport in Nairobi. I had met Richard before as he has been out to visit us in Nigeria quite a few times on business trips. I had not yet met his wife Sue though. It was after midnight when I landed and Richard drove us straight back to their lovely house. Sue had been asleep but got up to greet me and as we were due to have an early start the next morning, we didn't stay up chatting for too long before we all went to bed. I didn't have much chance to see their house that night but noted that it was one of the lovely old rambling stone-built ones with highly-polished old wooden floors. The bedroom I was sleeping in was beautiful. I was too excited to sleep much and it didn't seem to be long before the dawn broke and I awoke hearing strange 'hooping' calls from some large birds that were flying over the house. By the time I jumped out of bed to find out what they were, they had gone. The garden looked lovely in the early morning light and it was so refreshing to wake up to a cool bright morning after all the heat and humidity we are used to in the mornings in Nigeria. The climate is really lovely in Nairobi.

We had a three-hour drive ahead of us to the Mount Kenya Safari Lodge, so we set off very early. The countryside around us was open and vast. I was keen to see any signs of 'wild life' that I could but was somewhat disappointed when no great herds of elephant, lion or buffalo presented themselves on our journey. At one point on the drive, we saw a crowd of people in the road up ahead. I was sitting in the back of the Range Rover that Richard was driving so couldn't really see what was going on. Sue was a bit wary and just explaining to me that some students were protesting about something and seemed to have set up a road block for some reason, when Richard yelled to us to' hang on' and suddenly accelerated round all the traffic, scattering the crowds that were milling around. Sue was shouting at Richard to be careful when in the next instance huge stones and rocks were all being flung at the car by these people in an effort to make us stop. It was quite frightening for a few minutes, but Richard kept his foot down hard on the accelerator and we were soon out of range. He explained laughingly that if he had stopped we would probably have been lynched!

We eventually arrived at the Lodge, and it was really beautiful. Most of our party had already arrived on the previous evening. The main Lodge was a large white two-storey building with an enormous bay window where a vast restaurant and lounge looked out over acres of cultivated lawns, trees and flowering shrubs to a range of mountains, including Mount Kenya, in the distance. Within these grounds, set off *to one side were several bungalows where the guests stayed. I was sharing one with Graham and Pauline, as it contained two double bedrooms, two bathrooms, a large living room and kitchenette. Each one had a covered verandah in the front, furnished with sun-beds or swinging hammocks. White peacocks and crested cranes strolled around the grounds. The cranes were amazing birds, tall, grey and white colour, with beautiful red and black faces and a golden 'pom-pom' type of crest on the top of their heads. They were very tame and curious birds and even came right up to the windows and pecked on the glass panes to attract our attention! There was a nine hole golf course within the grounds and several of us played in the afternoon after lunch. We also played a few sets of tennis after that, before we showered and changed and went across to the restaurant to have dinner with the rest of the party.*

During the evening African Masai dancers, accompanied by rhythmical drummers, performed vigorously for us in the floodlit grounds. It was wonderful, later in the evening, to sit on the open verandas or by the huge log fires which were burning in the lovely old fireplaces, and listen to the unforgettable sounds of the African night. Also situated within the grounds was the Mount Kenya Game Ranch Animal Orphanage, which we visited the following morning. Here, many animals are cared for, that have been found abandoned or injured out in the bush, including baby elephants which have been orphaned because of the terrible, mindless slaughter of the beautiful adult elephants that is taking place, solely to furnish a flourishing ivory trade. These little orphans are now housed, fed, watered and treated here by resident veterinarians until it is deemed possible to re-introduce them back to the wild, or not, as the case may be.

The orphaned elephants are apparently very difficult to raise in captivity. They need intensive care day and night as they are very susceptible to pneumonia, enteritis and all manner of illness. The vets were telling us that it is difficult to find a milk formula to feed them with as it was discovered that they are allergic to cows' milk and elephant milk has so much more nutritive value which is essential for the survival of the babies. They were just beginning to realise also, that the baby elephants needed constant company both through the day and during the night and of course as they were usually looked after by their mothers and the herd while they were young, it was proving difficult to provide both the nourishment and the physical comfort in order to aide the survival of these beautiful creatures. Thankfully, things are improved somewhat but the elephant still remains a very endangered species, due mainly to the illegal poaching of the ivory.

Sadly, Brian missed the lovely weekend and arrived on the late flight on the Sunday night after we had all returned to Nairobi. We were staying with the Penfolds from then on, in their apartment for the rest of the week. Brian and Graham went off to the office every morning very early and we didn't see them again until late in the evenings, as the budget sessions were *intensive for everyone concerned. Pauline and I on the other hand had a lovely time. I was taken to play golf on beautiful courses with greens to putt on instead of browns and with long sweeping fairways bordered by pine trees instead of palm trees, lakes and water hazards, which we can't have in Nigeria because of the acute shortage of water, and fresh mountain air to breathe, as we were very high above sea level on some of the courses.*

The Muthaiga Club in Nairobi is a very old club, which was established in Colonial times, when women were forbidden to go into the bar. This still applies, would you believe, but we were allowed in the dining room for lunch or dinner at night. Dress is formal in the evenings and even at lunch-times the guests are not allowed to wear shorts or open-necked shirts. The Muthaiga Golf club, which is a completely separate entity, was slightly less formal but a certain dress code is still expected, and adhered to. We also played at Limuru and Karen Golf clubs which are very beautiful and more like English clubs than the African ones we are used to. One hole I remember which reminded me I was in East Africa though, was when we saw several women with heavy loads on their heads, running along a road which ran alongside the golf course. It never ceases to amaze me that these people can even walk without spilling their loads, let alone run. Their deportment and balance is superb.

Because Brian had missed the first weekend he managed to persuade the 'powers that be' to allow us to stay over the following weekend so that he could also enjoy a break after the budget sessions.   We were taken by the Penfolds and another couple, Dan and Betty Cassard, to the Tsavo National Game Park where we stayed overnight at the Kilaguni Lodge. Tsavo is a vast game park and famous for the large herds of elephant that live within it.   I can't tell you how wonderful it was, and so exciting, to sit on the balcony of our room as the sun went down, and to see the many herds of all varieties of game, coming in to the water holes that were situated just in front of the lodge to drink.   It was very hard to tear ourselves away and go to dinner.   After the meal we continued to watch far into the night, as various species; zebra, elephants, rhinoceros, etc. arrived to drink and we were even rewarded by a herd of buffalo at one point which was an absolutely amazing sight.   The animals almost seemed to come in to the water holes in turn and didn't seem to be put off by the fact that it was floodlit by this time.

The next morning we rose at 6am to head out for the Mzima springs.   Mount Kilimanjaro rose in the background, looking rather like a giant plum pudding covered with icing on the top, which was the snow of course, and is reputedly always present.   The Mzima Springs is a huge water hole where a herd of hippopotamus live.   It was a green oasis among the black lava formations that formed the mountain backdrop behind.   Incredibly, we were taken down some roughly hewn steps into a sort of cave below the water hole, which had large windows where we could stand and watch the hippos paddling around under the water. It was rather like a huge aquarium and the fact that we were so close to them was absolutely amazing and unforgettable. We returned to Kilaguni Lodge for breakfast and then moved on, driving through the game park spotting all sorts of different species of animals and birds, to Ngulia, where we stopped for a delicious lunch. Graham then drove us all the way back to Nairobi and because we hadn't seen any lions on our trip, he took us into the game park there to see if we could see any of the big cats. Sadly, we were unlucky on this trip as none were to be seen by us that day. The next day we had to leave and fly back to Nigeria, excited though, because Sally and Nick were arriving on the following day for their Easter holidays.

Thank you so much for collecting them from their schools once again, and taking them to the airport. I know what a toil it must be for you to do this but just want you to know how very much we appreciate all you do for us, and the children. I really don't know what we would do if you weren't around to help. They arrived safe and sound and it is so lovely to have them here with us again. We have found a spot at the end of the runway of the airport in Ikeja, which is out in the 'bush,' and where we can drive to in the car. We sit and wait until the plane lands almost in front of us, which is always a very tense moment! While we wait we listen to the night sounds of the crickets and a lovely tape of Neil Diamond playing softly in the car until the plane lands, and then while it is taxi-ing back to the terminal, we drive round to park the car before entering the usual chaos in the terminal where all the excited parents are waiting to pick up their children for the holidays.

We have so much planned for their holidays; trips to the beach and the Blue Elephant compound, where they have a pool and a golf course plus a bar of course! We have again organised the usual golf competitions for all the children who are out on holiday. Of course they are all practising madly at the moment as you can imagine. Nick is proving to be very good and the little Nigerian boys who caddy, all want to caddy for Nick as he is so small and can hit the ball a mighty long way for his size. Brian had some of your old clubs cut down to size for him Mum, and I have to say he has a very natural ability and can certainly whop the ball. Sally is also shaping up really well and has a lovely style. She can also really hit the ball well when she connects but tends to lose patience rather quickly I'm afraid. I think she would rather be in the pool with her chums than out on the golf course where it is always hot and sticky in this constant humidity. I shall let you know how they get on when next I write of course. Meanwhile, I must close now as it is getting late and time to get ready for dinner.

We are out again tonight for a barbecue at Mike and Ro's with their three girls. Mike has made a barbecue from half an oil drum which he fills with charcoal and then cooks on a grill on top. It is very effective and the kids love it too. We had a group of chums and their children around last Sunday for a 'sports day' at our house. We have a badminton court in the garden, as you know, and so the adults drew for partners for the day, and we had badminton matches, darts, putting (on the rug in the lounge) and table tennis matches against each other until the couple who had gained the most points in all the matches became the winners. It was great fun and plenty of booze and food was consumed throughout the day. We also organised games for the children, like egg and spoon, three legged, and sack races and hula-hoop competitions where they all joined in. Everyone was exhausted by the end but I think they all enjoyed it.

Will write again soon when I get a moment. This holiday is flying past all too quickly as always and we dread the thought of putting them on the plane back to school again.

All our love to you all

As Always

Maureen Brian Sally and Nick.xxx

CHAPTER 14 - JAPANESE EVENING

Around this time, we had quite a large Japanese contingent in Ikeja who had become members of the golf club. They all worked in the light engineering industries in Ikeja, of which there were many. One of our members, a Mr. Hasegawa, spoke good English and so became a sort of spokesman for the others. He was a managing director of one of the companies, was a perfect gentleman and a very good golfer. It was obvious that the majority of his fellow countrymen, some of whom he employed, would not be able to join in with all our golf competitions as they had neither the skills nor the language and there would have been too many people competing on the small nine hole course if they had. He encouraged them to learn however, and asked permission for them to hold their own competitions sometimes, which he would then organise and control. In return for this the Japanese members and their wives asked if they could host an evening at the club for the rest of the club members. It turned out to be an amazing evening. We duly arrived at the club at about six o'clock, before it went dark, to be greeted by an enormous hardboard cut-out of a Japanese Shinto Shrine painted red and black which had been erected at the top of the steps leading up to the terrace. As we passed under the shrine, we were met by some of the wives who were all beautifully dressed in their national costume and some in full Kimono, offering us plates of exquisitely prepared Japanese food to have with an aperitif of Saki. We had not met the wives of most of the men before as they never came to the club and only socialised among themselves. Mrs Hasegawa came occasionally with her husband as she also played golf and spoke some English. They were all so charming and polite and the food was absolutely delicious. The Japanese ladies circulated constantly offering tiny morsels of exquisite food, bowing after every offering and making sure everyone had everything they needed to eat and drink.

After we had all eaten, the entertainment began. The men had rigged up a record player and put some music on. First of all the ladies performed some traditional Japanese dancing which was slow and precise with many head and hand movements, all of which meant something I'm sure, as they were obviously telling a story. Then one of the men took the centre stage and put on another record, playing Japanese music. Taking a microphone in his hand he started accompanying the music by 'singing' (arguably) a low rumbling sound which gradually rose to a peak of the most extraordinary high pitched warbling noise that he squeezed out of his throat while his eyes were closed and his face was contorted into what looked like incredible pain. We were all quite mesmerised, not knowing whether it was supposed to be funny or deadly serious, we didn't know if we should laugh or cry. I remember the small child of a friend of ours just standing in front of the man gazing up into the man's contorted face, with a look of absolute fascination! After he had finally finished, we all applauded loudly of course, and that seemed to open the floodgates, as many more of the men then took their turn with the microphone and 'sang' for our entertainment. I'm glad to say that some of them sang to more modern pop music so that we could all join in and I suppose it was the first time we had experienced a sort of 'Karaoke' evening with which we are now all familiar.

Another of Mr. Hasegawa's associates, a Mr. Matsui, was also a very good golfer and he eventually joined in with our competitions. He hardly spoke any English, but had learnt to say 'Good Shot!' after every hit, which amused everyone greatly. He started winning many of the silver trophies that had been donated to the club by some of the large companies in Ikeja, and which were played for annually. One day, he arrived at the club with a new silver cup that he presented to our Captain and made clear that he wished to donate it to the club. What we didn't know then was that Mr. Matsui had been posted back to Japan, and he left the following week, taking all the club trophies that he had won that year with him! Nobody could blame him really as it obviously hadn't been made clear to him that he had to return them to the club to be played for again the following year!

After the very successful Japanese evening, the Nigerian members of the club decided that they would also like to organise an evening providing food and entertainment for the other members. We duly arrived on the set evening and were treated to a red hot West African curry, made with all sorts of meats that we didn't like to enquire too closely what they were! Suffice it to say that many bones, including whole jaw bones, and teeth of various animals were left on the sides of many plates that evening. They showed us how to take a portion of fu fu or moin-moin and roll it up into a ball with the fingers of the hand, opposite to the one used to attend to your personal hygiene, before dipping it into the curry or stew and then popping it into your mouth! We were also asked to leave room for a special Nigerian delicacy that hadn't been delivered to the golf club on time, but which they were sure would turn up sometime during the evening. When it did finally arrive, it turned out to be a stew of the small crabs that we had all seen on the beaches. All the shells, legs and claws were still floating around in the pepper-hot juices that the crabs had been cooked in. Along with the fu-fu which is made from beans and moin-moin that is cassava based and served with most of the food they eat, we were served drinks of palm wine which is made from the fermented juices of the special palm nuts, and is extremely potent! The evening continued with everyone dancing the Highlife until well into the early hours of the morning.

The indiginisation programme which General Gowan had introduced several years before he was ousted, was now beginning to take effect. After the Biafran War, Nigeria discovered oil and slowly enjoyed an economic upturn. This also meant a rapid increase in corruption most notably by federal government officials. General Gowan had decided that because of the discovery of oil, many sectors of the Nigerian economy no longer needed foreign investment and introduced an indiginisation decree which greatly benefitted and just happened to provide windfall gains to many well connected Nigerians but was to prove highly detrimental to other companies that were not connected to the oil industries. Increased wealth resulted in fake import licences being issued. This corrupt practice at one time in 1975 saw 20 million tons of cement waiting to be unloaded from ships which were waiting outside Lagos harbour. The ships were sitting for months on end, miles outside the entrance to the port and ended up eventually blocking essential supplies from being able to get in. Shippers and suppliers 'jumped on the bandwagon' and all were collecting millions of dollars in demurrage charges of 4000 US Dollars per day while their ships sat waiting to be unloaded. It was money for 'old rope'! Civilian pilots took to flying out over the sea to give passengers on night flights the opportunity to view the hundreds of ships waiting down below in the shipping lanes outside the harbour. The twinkling lights which were reflected in the water from all the waiting vessels, made it look like another enormous city. This 'blockade' lasted some two years during which time much of the cement in the ships actually solidified and some of the ships were just 'old tubs' that were picking up the fees and not fit to put to sea, so ended up being 'scuttled' in the harbour by some unscrupulous owners.

In July 1975 while General Gowan was attending an OAU Summit in Kampala a bloodless coup took place in Lagos and Brigadier Murtala Mohammed was declared as the new Head of State. Gowan subsequently went into exile in UK where he studied and acquired a Phd in Political Science at Warwick University.

Livestock Feeds Ltd.
PMB 1097
Ikeja

Jan. 1976

Dearest All.
Thank you so much for your letter which we received yesterday. So pleased to hear you had picked the children up from the airport and delivered them to their schools again. We always worry until we hear from you that they arrived safely. The holiday passed all too quickly as usual and it never gets any easier to put them back on that plane. It was a shame that it had to be on my Birthday too. It was wonderful to have had them back here for Christmas though and we all enjoyed it enormously.
We have just had quite an exciting week as we had the MCC touring team out in Ikeja. Among the players were Colin Cowdrey, Bob Barber and Ted Clarke. The WAAC sports club in Ikeja was transformed into a cricket ground for the week. The old wooden hut was made into a pavilion and even had a little white picket fence placed around it. The cricket pitch, which was situated in the sports field where the first two holes of golf and the rugby ground is, had to be made out of a special sort of matting because of course the grass is very different here. As

195

there was no place for the teams to shower, change or eat in the 'Pavilion,' the girls from the golf club were asked if they could provide the lunch at the golf club for the teams every day plus about 50 officials and invited guests. It was quite a challenge as you can imagine. We were also really handicapped at the time because the power was very sporadic and we had been having major power cuts for about a week.

We girls decided that we would provide a running buffet every lunch time and we all had to prepare the dishes in our own homes every morning, or do the cooking when there was power, and bring them up to the club in time to set it all up for lunch. It all worked extremely well in the end and we got to meet and get to know all the players. The members of the golf club committee were also asked to entertain two members of the team from the MCC, plus our own friends if we liked, every evening for dinner, as it was deemed they would be far happier in our homes with company, rather than sitting in the airport hotel on their own. They were certainly a lively crowd I can tell you and we all got on very well. We ended up having a barbecue and dance at the golf club on their last night, which the cricket team hosted, to thank us all for our magnificent efforts over the week. It was all good fun and I have to say we were quite surprised at how appreciative some of the older Nigerian members were. They would go to watch the cricket every day and instead of wearing their traditional Nigerian robes, were usually dressed in flannels and blazers and

196

yes, you've guessed it, a panama hat! I suspect they were the Nigerians who had been educated in the UK, as cricket isn't normally played here. It's a great pity that Nick wasn't here as he would have loved it. We did get a programme for him though, which all the team members autographed.

Brian is working flat out at the moment as the guys from New York are coming next month for the opening of the new pharmaceutical plant in Ikeja. Again, the Pfizer ladies are expected to entertain the wives who will be accompanying the boss men so we are planning an itinerary for that at the moment.

Will close now and hope that you and all the family are keeping well.

Our love to all and many thanks again for collecting and delivering Sally and Nick,

As Always.

Maureen and Brian.xxxx

CHAPTER 15 - THE GHANA SAGA

Pfizer had been building a brand new Pharmaceutical plant in Ikeja during most of the previous year so that certain drugs, pills and potions could at last be manufactured in Nigeria instead of having to import them all.

There was also the new pre-mix Plant on the Agricultural side, in which Brian had been heavily involved with doing the feasibility studies, plus all the budgeting projections and overseeing of the building which was going to be in operation the next year.   A new American boss had come to take over in Nigeria by then and this one was a really good guy whom we had known for a couple of years previously when he had visited Nigeria from Nairobi, where he was working for Pfizer at the time.   Richard and his wife Sue were younger than the previous American MD, who had tried but failed to come to terms with conditions in Nigeria and had therefore returned to the States with his wife.   Richard and Sue were a lovely couple and we soon became friends.

One of the first highlights of their term in Nigeria was to be the opening of the new Pharmaceutical plant which was nearing completion in Ikeja.

Livestock Feeds Ltd.
PMB. 1097
Ikeja
Lagos State

Feb 1976

Dearest All

   The grand opening of the new pharmaceutical plant has at last taken place at the beginning of the month. So you can imagine, we have all been very busy organising the itinerary for the visiting personnel, which had to be perfect, right down to the last detail!

   The Vice President of Pfizer International flew in from New York, with several of the Directors and their wives, in one of the Pfizer private jets. Also invited were all the major personnel from Nairobi, plus their wives, along with many Nigerian State Governors, Tribal Chieftains, and visiting hierarchy.

   On the grand opening day we all sat in front of the splendid new building under canvas awnings in fierce heat while all the speeches were made, and the plant was finally opened by Colonel Dan Suleman who is the Federal Minister for Health in Nigeria. After the tape had been cut, we were all invited to go on a conducted tour to the parts of the plant where we were allowed to go without having to get dressed from head to toe in protective overalls, head gear and goggles!

   It had been decided that the Pfizer wives in Ikeja were to entertain the wives of the American directors

199

during the three days of their visit. On the first day we took them down to Lagos to visit the Museum. We all set off in selected company cars with drivers. The American women simply could not believe that it took an hour and a half to drive the fourteen miles to Lagos. We secretly thought it would be good for them to see the state of the traffic and the congestion that occurs daily on the infamous Ikorodu Road. They were amazed of course and quite as shocked, as I remember I had been on my first visit to Lagos.

After our quiet visit looking round the museum, which didn't take long as there was little to see other than the old carvings and Benin Bronze heads and masks, we visited a school for blind children nearby. This is run as a charity by two lovely white Irish Catholic Sisters, who care for and house about 70 very young children. These children live permanently at the school and are taught to read Braille. When they are old enough, they learn to type on a few battered old Braille typewriters that have at some time in the past, been purloined from some kind benefactor. The Sisters are marvellous and try to make the children as independent as possible so that they learn to fend for themselves, and fight and play as normal children do. I will never forget seeing two tiny four year old children who were totally blind, with no light perception whatsoever, running confidently across the playground towards the sisters who were calling them by name and clapping their hands so that they could hear the sound, and then when they got to the other side, clapping themselves and laughing with sheer joy at their own accomplishment. I have to say we all found it to be a very moving and emotional experience that morning. To think that most of these innocent little children had been abandoned by their parents because they were blind was absolutely heartbreaking.

When we finally got home through the traffic we only had time to change quickly, before going all the way back to Lagos again for an evening reception at the American Embassy, where we had to stand for another four hours, meeting and making polite conversation with all the other invited guests. This round of entertaining and visits continued without a break, for three days and nights.

One morning we were given a guided tour of the Pfizer Gulf Stream jet that had brought the Vice President and his entourage to Lagos and had been 'parked' at the airport in Ikeja. It is a fabulous little plane. The seats inside the cabin were all comfortable leather arm chairs with tables in between that could be used for their meals or conference facilities.

On the final day, all the women went on a boat trip around Lagos Harbour and then on to one of the beaches on the other side of the lagoon. I nearly cracked up with laughter when the boat that we were on, went through the place where they tip all the night soil into the lagoon and horror of horrors, the propeller fouled up and the engine stopped. There we were in this small boat in the middle of all this foul smelling excreta which was floating all around us in the water! Thankfully, the boat boys cleared the stuff (don't ask what it was!) that had wrapped around the propeller, and we were able to get across to the beach. I can tell you that by then the American wives just couldn't wait to get away!

Our last visit on that day was at their request, to go to one of the markets in Lagos. Maybe they had imagined something completely different but I don't think they were quite prepared for what they found when they had to walk, in all their finery, during the fiercest heat of the day, through all the filth and flies and stinking rubbish that was in the market.

We came to the medicine man's stall where all the shrunken monkeys' heads, skulls of all shapes and sizes, chicken heads and feet, red tail feathers of the West African Grey parrots, and goodness knows what else they use in their Ju-Ju potions, were laid out for us to see! I'm sure they thought it was all very interesting but I think they were all quite relieved to get back to their privileged lives in the United States.

As a sort of 'Thank-you' for all the hard work that had been put in for that visit and the fact that Sue and I had done some posters for the Pfizer products which were to be on display at the Trade Fair, due to be held in Accra Ghana the following week, Richard decided that Sue and I might like to accompany Brian and himself who were going over to the Trade fair for a couple of days. I was really looking forward to it as Brian had told me many times how different Ghana is to here.

We set off by air, early on February 12th and arrived in Ghana in time to drive straight to the Trade Fair in Accra before lunch. The stands were very interesting and Pfizer had two, one of which had an incubator where the people could watch the chickens being hatched. This proved to be a great draw for the visiting crowds. The Ghanaians are a very colourful and cheerful race. They seem to have a good standard of education and the towns all appear to be clean and well-kept. There are excellent restaurants in Accra, as food is flown in from Paris and elsewhere on a daily basis. This seemed to be rather strange to us, as there was very little to buy in the shops and markets. Lieutenant Colonel Acheampong took over the country in a bloodless coup in 1972 and in an attempt to solve the economic problems has, along with other changes of policy, re-valued the currency, nationalized foreign companies, allowed the imports of certain foods while at the same time trying to encourage agricultural independence. This policy, along with several others that he has decreed, isn't working, and Ghana is falling very seriously into greater financial debt. We, on the other hand relished the lovely meals we had at Edwards, a charming restaurant we went to for lunch and also the superb Palm Court Chinese restaurant where we had dinner that night, and which is situated in a magnificent location overlooking the ocean.

The following morning, Friday 13th by the way, after Richard and Brian had left for the office in Accra, a car was sent back for Sue and me and we went down to the Makola market. This is a very *orderly, clean and well-organised market. Sections are taken up with the display of various traditional cloths, trade beads, fruit and fish, etc. The women all have bright stalls of uniform size which are provided by the Government and those who are not able to pay the minimal rent for a stall, are allowed to sit in the front of the stalls at long low tables. Instead of having a canopy over their heads, they each wear a straw hat with an enormous brim which keeps the sun off their bodies as well as their wares! The usual mode of dress for the Ghanaian women is a short sleeved cotton jacket and long skirt in the traditionally colourful Java wax prints. The men wear a boubou on important occasions, which is a length of cloth, worn like a Togo, with the very finest ones being hand woven in heavy silk and cotton in their traditional designs and colours.*

In the afternoon, we went to Tema and were driven around the port which is just outside the town. We then went to the old fishing port which was very busy with crowds of people all waiting for the gaily painted dug-out canoes to arrive so that they could inspect and buy the latest catch. It was very interesting to see first the modern port with a fleet of trawlers, cargo ships, even a passenger cruiser, with all the equipment for loading and unloading passengers and cargo, on one side and then on the other side of the port the old canoes, which had been hewn by hand out of old tree trunks. These canoes, were skillfully manoeuvered by two or three men, who timed the crest of the waves to the second to enable them to come crashing up the beach on a mighty wave. Then, with many hands at the ready, to make light work of hauling the boat with 'the catch' up the beach, the fish could either be sold fresh, or was spread out on the shore to be salted and dried in the sun. The old fishing port was absolutely crowded with people and activity, but the new port was strangely silent and almost deserted.

After watching the return of the fishermen for a while, we drove on, up to Legon Hill to visit the University of Ghana. This overlooks the city of Accra. The buildings there were rather Spanish looking with white walls, red tiled roofs and wooden doors and shutters. It was beautifully laid out with all the faculties lining a long driveway which led up to a clock tower on the top of the hill. We were very impressed. We moved on to visit Achimota College, which was quite near-by. This was the first Secondary School to be built in Ghana and was also beautifully laid out and well maintained. The buildings were all painted white with blue shutters and looked very Colonial in style. We noticed that there were still expatriate teachers working there. Sadly, we couldn't linger as Sue and I had been invited to take afternoon tea with Mrs Annee who is a lovely Ghanaian person who works at the Pfizer office in Accra.

When we arrived at her very spacious modern house at 5 o'clock, we were greeted with the words 'What has been happening in your country then?' We had no idea what she was talking about! She told us 'There has been a coup in Nigeria!' and she had heard it over the radio.   When Richard and Brian arrived back at the hotel that evening they told us that the airports had been closed and there were no flights into or out of Nigeria so we could not return home the next day as planned!   We later discovered that the Head of State of Nigeria, General Murtala Mohammed had been killed while he was in his car in Lagos and the leader of the coup had been one Colonel Dimka, who was the physical training instructor for the Army in Lagos.   The coup had been crushed after some fighting and skirmishes and the new head of State in Nigeria was declared to be General Olesegun Obasanjo.   Meanwhile, we were stranded in Accra. It could have been a lot worse I suppose!   That evening, Emmanuel Asiedu, the manager of Pfizer pharmaceuticals in Accra, took us all to a wonderful Swiss restaurant called "Le Chevalier" for dinner. The food was excellent, though expensive, the decor was Swiss and the waiters, who are Ghanaian, all wear traditional Swiss costume, which looks a little odd in Accra I have to admit.

The following morning, Richard had arranged a meeting so Brian drove Sue and I out to Aburi, a village in the Akwapim hills, to visit the Botanical gardens there.   These had been started in Colonial days by a British graduate who had sadly died after spending only five years in the country and it had then been taken on by another British person who had only lasted four years before he too died, probably, it is thought from the dreaded Malaria, which was the

206

biggest killer in West Africa in those days. The gardens survived, however, and are still very beautiful. The nurseries are full of interesting plants and different species of rare and wonderful orchids. We only wished we could have taken some of them with us back to Nigeria.

Richard joined us for lunch as we weren't going to be able to get back to Nigeria that day, and afterwards we all headed off to see the Akosombo Dam. This is approximately 50 miles north of Accra on the Volta river. It forms one of the largest artificial lakes in the world. During the construction of the dam, part of the Volta river basin was flooded, which subsequently created the Volta Lake. It was originally intended to service the aluminium industry in Ghana. The cost of all this is escalating at an alarming rate and the World Bank, together with other American Banks and private companies, have been trying for years to help Ghana to finance the project which never seems to fully get off the ground. We viewed the lake from the balcony of the new Volta Hotel which overlooks the Dam but unfortunately, were not allowed to go any closer. It had been raining on our way up to the Lake and so was rather dull that day but we felt it would normally be a magnificent sight in the sunlight as it was bounded by rocky crags and beautiful scenery as far as the eye could see.

Later that evening we had dinner at "The Blow-Up Restaurant" which was supposed to be the 'wildest discotheque in town' on a Saturday night, or so we were led to believe! We 'hung around' until midnight but there still didn't seem to be much action so we moved on to the old Star Hotel where the Highlife was in full swing. This was a fantastic scene. Crowds of people were there, with a live band, playing very loud but excellent music, a comic character who sang like 'Satchmo' (Louis Armstrong) and literally everyone seemed to be dancing. They were dancing a version of the highlife that seems to have been updated and modernized as it was far more lively than the one which we see danced in Nigeria. The Ghanaians love to dance and even if they had no partners, the music had such an effect on them that they just had to get up and dance. The waiters were dancing in odd corners when they weren't serving drinks, the children, waiting for their parents, all joined in the dancing, even the people watching, including us, were all swaying and tapping their feet to the hypnotic rhythm of the music. It was really lively and fun and we had a marvelous time.

The next day, being Sunday, we knew there would be no planes anyway so we decided to go for a drive up the coast and see some of Ghana's famous old fortresses. There are 32 forts and castles along the coast, all erected by various countries that used to trade with West Africa. The oldest castle on the coast was built by the Portuguese at Elmina in 1482. We could only go as far as Cape Coast that day. This one was built originally by the Swedish traders in 1653, later seized by the Danes and then conquered by the English in 1664 when it was extensively rebuilt and became the seat of the Colonial Government of the British Gold Coast. The main items of trade in those times were the exportation of timber and gold to Europe and African slaves to America. We found it to be a fascinating place. The building was perched on the edge of a rocky promontory overlooking the magnificent coastline. There are still old cannon guns pointing out to sea from the terrace above the rocks. Its castellated walls are painted white which was dazzling in the bright sunlight. In stark contrast were the deep, dank dungeons beneath, which had been created to house the thousands of poor slaves who were kept, sometimes for months while awaiting the next ship, chained and shackled, and lying side by side, so closely bound that they were unable to move. They were kept like rats in total darkness, lying in their own excrement, while the governor lived in his stately apartments above, which looked out over the beautiful bay. We were able to go into the building and dungeons as the Ghanaians are trying to make it into a sort of Museum and so we had a guide, a charming woman who showed us around and told us a little about the history. Apparently, the bricks that lined the dungeons had been imported from England all those years ago.

The floors were being excavated in one of the dungeons and the horrible black greasy stuff that we were walking on had been scraped away at one point to find some ten inches below it the bricks and drainage channels of the original floor. What had built up over the years during the slave trade was the waste food and *excreta of the slaves, bat-poo and goodness knows what else! The shackles that the slaves wore round their feet and necks were still being found in the floors and walls of the dungeons. There were also some bones found of the poor unfortunates who had died before they ever left the dungeons. Even when they were on board the ships bound for America, they were still shackled and packed like sardines in the bowels of the vessels for weeks on end. It was a horrible and gruesome tale. Part of the building is still being used as a prison and although our guide asked us kindly not to go near the wall and gaze down upon the prisoners, we couldn't help turning to catch a glimpse of them through the battlements in the wall. At least these men were in an open yard in the fresh air and sunshine and not tied up in those awful black dungeons below.*

Later, whilst on our way back to Accra, we stopped at another village along the coast called Winneba. Here, the castle had crumbled and gone, but as we drove down to a beautiful stretch of bay, we encountered a really busy and lively scene. Among the rocks and the surf, the fishing canoes were paddling in by the dozens. The beach was also lined from one end to the other with dug-out canoes and wooden fishing boats, all traditionally carved and decorated with brightly coloured paints and dyes. The far end of the beach was crowded with people, so being curious, we got out of the car and walked along the beach to see what was happening. The stench of the drying fish that assailed our nostrils, was appalling at first. This is one smell I am never going to get used to!

We picked our way among the canoes and the piles of fish that had been spread out to dry, until we came to the crowds who were all standing looking at something by the rocks at the far end of the bay. As we drew nearer, we could hear chanting and the pulsating sound of drums and sticks being played. We had to stand on tiptoe to see through the crowd of people and came upon a truly amazing sight. A young girl was running round in a circle swinging a large curved sword around and around her head, changing it from one hand to the other on the completion of every swing. Another young girl, looking dazed and confused, was sitting in the middle of the circle, clad only in a loin cloth and she was covered in sand. For one horrible moment, we thought they were going to sacrifice the girl in the centre, we all held our breath in disbelief. After a while the girl tried to get up and began staggering and rolling down the beach until she finally fell into the sea. Had she been injured? We couldn't tell. Meanwhile, other young girls were taking it in turns to run round in the circle swinging the sword above their heads. Some of them became completely hypnotised by this, and went into a trance, some looked as if they were having a fit, or behaved as if they were completely drunk and were staggering about all over the place. We asked an elderly Ghanaian man who was standing nearby, what was going on but he looked at us, the only four white people on that beach, and said quietly,

'It is a Rite.' I would have loved to have taken some photographs but suddenly we felt as if we were intruding on something where we had no business to be, we felt as if we were prying into something that didn't belong to us. We turned and slipped quietly back to the car.

I have often thought that these tribal 'rites' where people go into a frenzy or a trance, when spirits are supposed to enter the person's body and possess them, may have been exaggerated or even 'faked' altogether. Physically seeing it there before us, didn't seem as if it was faked. A more feasible explanation probably is that these young girls were celebrating puberty, or some such time in their teenage lives, and they had been conditioned to believe that this is what would happen to them and in their intense excitement and anticipation, it actually did send them into a trance. We shall never know for sure but whatever it was, it was strange to see it really happening before us; and oddly enough, it felt quite a privilege to have witnessed it too.

For the next week, Brian and Richard tried to work at the office in Accra while Sue and I played at being the tourists and with the help of a car and driver explored the regions near Accra, visiting the University again, browsing in their bookshop, visiting expatriates whom we knew from Lagos or Ikeja, going to the Achimota Golf club and one day to a pottery where we stayed to watch the men making some very good pots. That was very interesting. We walked into a tiny *walled compound and once again were overwhelmed by the stench from the pits where they kept the grey clay. I must have a very sensitive nose! We felt sure they must have mixed manure with the clay. Two or three red earth kilns stood at the far end of the compound. These were rather like old-fashioned bee hives, but larger of course. In one of the rooms at the side, three men were sitting at their very home-made wooden wheels, leisurely shaping the pots as they treadled the wheels rhythmically with their feet. There never seems to be any hurry in Ghana. It all looked very relaxing and I would have loved to have had a go. We looked at the wares on display on the shelves in the other room and found them to be rather tasteful, nothing fine or delicate but ample-sized coffee cups or mugs in grey, brown or blue glazes, lovely soup bowls in dark browns and chunky jugs in all shapes and sizes. It was all very interesting and if it hadn't been for the awful smell pervading the atmosphere, I would have liked to have stayed longer and watch the potters at work.*

During that week we also met up with quite a few people whom we know from Ikeja, who had been out of Nigeria on business trips to UK or Europe when the coup happened and who, like us, had been unable to get back to Nigeria as the airports were all still closed. Our hotel was filling up with people who thought that by being in Accra, they would be the first to get back to Lagos. Most of these men had left wives and children in Nigeria and of course were worried sick about their safety. Communications and news coming out of Nigeria were scant to say the least. Brian and Richard were lucky to have radio connection with the Ikeja office and by speaking in some sort of 'code' language were able to keep some vague 'tabs' on what was really going on in the country. They used to say things like, 'What's the climate like in Lagos today?' The reply might be 'Its quite calm but cloudy today!' or 'Stormy' if there was any rioting in the capital!

Meanwhile, the Hotel laundry in Accra was working overtime to try to keep up with the fact that we had only brought enough clothes for two days and there was absolutely nothing to buy in the shops. One night Sue said to me 'Maureen I'm so bored with wearing the same dress every night, shall we swap dresses tonight?' which we duly did, and it was quite hilarious but felt good. Luckily we were about the same size! It was quite a laugh. We were all fed up with going up to the airport everyday, only to be turned away with no news again. Our evenings were quite good fun as we were meeting up with increasingly more people that we knew and either going to a restaurant or being entertained in the homes of old friends who now lived in Accra. One evening we met Pele the famous footballer from Brazil, who was dining in the same restaurant as us at the airport. Richard went over to him to ask how he had managed to get out of Nigeria, as we knew that he had been visiting the Nigerian football team just before the coup. It appeared that he had eventually been allowed to hire a

214

private jet to fly him to Accra so that he could catch another flight to London from where he could go back to join his team in Brazil. This was not before he had been subjected to endless interrogation and searches, in spite of the fact that the Nigerian people normally revered him and treated him as some sort of god.

One day when Richard and Brian had no commitments at the office, we decided to go up the coast again and have a day on a beach that had been recommended to us. We took a trip into the town first to see if we could get any food to take with us for a picnic. The shops were sadly lacking in food and commodities as there were no imports allowed into the shops at this time. We thought that probably most essentials could be found if one knew where to look for them and were prepared to pay the black market price. All we could get from the shops however was some bread, tomatoes, onions, carrots, fried plantain, pineapple, and some bananas. There was no butter, cheese, ham or tinned meats available. We bought some avocado pears to spread on our bread in lieu of butter. We drove some thirteen miles or so out to the beach hut that our friend had said we could use for the afternoon. This turned out to be only a thatched parasol in reality but it did at least provide some shade. We locked all our things in the boot of the car as our friend Chet had warned us not to leave the car open or anything lying around. He even warned us not to go into the sea at the same time without leaving someone always 'on guard' by the hut. We bought four coconuts from a woman who was collecting them from the trees round about and she chopped the tops off so that we could drink the liquid inside and then eat the delicious soft flesh within. It was a superb beach, almost deserted. The tide was rapidly coming in, so we sat just in front of the parasol, watching the magnificent surf. Our pic-nic was delicious and we gave the remainder of the bread to the children of the woman who had sold us the coconuts, as they were still hanging around, obviously waiting for scraps. We took it in turns to splash around in the waves at the edge of the shore. We had no swimming gear with us of course and the beach shelved very steeply so it would have been quite dangerous to go in too deep anyway as the undertow was very strong.

When it was time for us to leave, I went to get my things out of the boot of the car, which we had parked just behind the parasol in the shade of the coconut trees. I couldn't open the lid. I noticed that it had a very large dent in the middle of the boot lid that hadn't been there before, and thought at first that a coconut must have dropped on it. The others joined me and we decided that it couldn't possibly have been a coconut as the dent in the middle would have needed a much heavier object to have forced it up at one side like that. We finally managed to open the lid and were aghast at what we saw. The boot had been ransacked! We couldn't believe our eyes. The boot lid had obviously been forced up at one side, just wide enough for an arm to get inside. All the contents of Sue's handbag and mine had been spilled all over the boot.

Our clothes were all screwed up and there was loose change all over the place.   Sue had lost $300 of travellers cheques, 30 Cedis (Ghanaian currency) and 10 Naira (Nigerian).   Both hers and Richard's international driving licences had been torn up. Richard's watch which had been brand new at Christmas, had disappeared and when Richard looked in the pocket of his trousers, which had been hanging in the beach hut, all his money had gone from his wallet.   By some curious quirk of fate, Brian's watch and mine, my purse, my camera and all the contents of my handbag, even though it had been tipped out into the boot of the car, were all still there.   Brian had decided to leave his wallet in our hotel room so fortunately didn't have it with him and even though the pockets of his trousers were turned inside out in the car, nothing had been in them in the first place. It was quite bizarre.   As there was no police station in this remote part of the country, Richard and Brian decided that the best policy would be to demand an audience with the Chieftain of the village and to report that there was a thief in their midst.

We went to where there was a collection of small thatched wooden huts and they spoke to a man in pidgin-english who understood enough to go and summon the chief.   We then continued to wait for a long time until the Chief and all the village elders had been contacted, arrived and assembled, now dressed in their fine Ghanaian silk boubous, in the largest of the huts in the small village, which was obviously the 'meeting house.'   The Chief sat on a carved Ashanti

217

Stool, denoting his authority, while the rest of the elders including Richard and Brian, either stood or sat around in a half circle on the earth floor. There were no windows in the room but just the open doorway where the light came in. They related our story to the assembled company amid much 'ooh-ing and ah-ing, umbalah-ing, gesturing and arm waving, until it became fairly heated. Unfortunately, not much English was spoken, so it was difficult to know whether it was genuinely understood or not. It became obvious though, that nothing was going to be done about it. The Chief just summed it up and eventually said through his interpreters, that unfortunately some people lived like that. There had been no witnesses, so nobody in the village could be blamed. It had been a sheer waste of a couple of hours. We left, thoroughly disappointed at the outcome. We still couldn't quite believe that it had happened almost in front of our very noses. We were only sitting a few yards in front of the car and the parasol. It must have been the sheer noise of the surf pounding up the beach that masked any noise from the robbery. On reflection, we wondered if it was possible for the thieves to have forced the boot lid up just enough for the children to have got their arms through, which may have explained why some of the contents of the handbags, even though they had been tipped out in the boot, were just beyond their reach. On the way back to the hotel that evening, we called at the first police station in one of the towns that we passed through, but nothing was ever followed up.

We didn't really expect it to be, but just reporting it made us feel a bit better.

We were desperately hot and thirsty on the long drive back and when we came up behind an old 'mammy wagon' heaped full of pineapples with some of the women who had been cutting them in the plantations sitting on top, we drove up behind, gesturing and begging them to stop. They eventually understood and we then bought some pineapples, with the change that had been left in the boot of the car. The women peeled and sliced them for us. I can honestly say that they were the most sweet and deliciously refreshing pineapples we had ever tasted!

The next four days were spent going up to the airport every morning to see if there was any hope of us getting back that day. When we realised there were still no planes being allowed into Nigeria, we tried to occupy ourselves as best we could. We visited a small village called Medina where we watched the women tying the cloths in preparation for the dying process. Many of the resulting designs were very attractive and interesting. We visited the Achimota Golf club several more times and visited friends old and new in their homes. When we eventually heard that Nigeria had re-opened its borders at last, we all flocked up to the airport in readiness for the first flight out. After hearing that we were not going to get a plane that day, we had to retire back to the hotel for the umpteenth time, disappointed yet again.

The chaos at the airport in Ghana was just as bad as Nigeria. No one formed an orderly queue. It *was a case of everyone for themselves. Masses of people were fighting and shouting, pushing and shoving, in order to ensure a place at the front near the check-in desk. We even saw people being lifted over other people's heads and passed along high in the air to try to get near the desk. It was quite alarming and Sue and I didn't really relish joining in the scrum. Finally, ten days after we had arrived in Accra for a two day visit, Nigeria sent planes to Ghana to 'rescue' all those passengers who had been stranded there for the duration of the coup in Lagos. It had certainly been an interesting visit, but we were all very glad to get back home again, if only so that we could change our clothes at last!*

Because we had such a long stay in Accra, we only had one day back at home before Brian was off again, this time to a Pfizer meeting in Athens.
I had been invited to stay with Pauline in Nairobi while he was away, as her husband Graham was going to Athens as well. I flew out to Nairobi and had a wonderful week with Pauline. We played golf on some beautiful courses with proper greens and lovely fairways that in some cases were bordered by trees other than palm trees. The following weekend, Pauline and I had been invited to go to Taita Hills and Salt Lick Game Lodge with a Dr. Bill Osbourne, an Australian chap, who worked for Pfizer. Salt Lick was amazing. We stayed there overnight in thatched round huts, which were built up on stilts and overlooked the water hole where the animals came up to drink. At night it

was floodlit so you could watch all night if you so desired. There was also a tunnel leading from the hotel down to the water hole which came out into a little room which had barred windows just above ground level so that you could watch the animals at extremely close quarters. It was very exciting when the elephants came in and you were watching at just about their knee height right in the middle of the herd. To stare one in the eye when they bent their heads to drink was quite breathtaking. The next day Bill drove us round part of Tsavo and Ngulia game parks and we stopped at Kilagoonie Lodge for lunch which was fantastic. We saw everything except the big cats which was slightly disappointing but hopefully there will be another time.

I arrived back in Nigeria the following Friday evening, just about the same time that Brian arrived back from Athens too. We went straight out to a party at the Casa Pepe and then had to be up really early the next morning to drive up to Ibadan for an inter-club golf match which lasted over the weekend. Two rounds of eighteen holes plus a barbecue dinner and dance on the Saturday evening.

Quite an exhausting time of late as you can see and so I really must close now and catch up on some sleep!

Sending lots of love to you and all the family.

As Always

Brian and Maureen.xxxx

Livestock Feeds Ltd.
PMB 1097
Ikeja
Lagos State
Nigeria

February 1977

My Dear All.

Just had a very exhausting month, so sorry I haven't been able to write for a week or two as we've been very busy moving house! We were rather annoyed and somewhat upset when our landlord, Harold Sodipo, decided he wanted our house for one of his nephews to live in, and he wanted it very quickly! We were fortunate I suppose, in that another couple from Pfizer have been posted to work in Nairobi and so were due to leave their house in Ikeja very shortly and as the lease was still operational, we could move straight into that house. The sad part is, that it is on what is known as 'the Industrial Estate' in Ikeja, where all the factories and offices are situated. Our house on Harold Sodipo Crescent in the GRA has been really lovely for us for the past six years as most of our friends lived near us and we were also very close to the Country Club and Golf Club as you know, where most of our socialising is done.

The plus side I suppose, is that Brian will be very close to his office and as the traffic in Ikeja is getting increasingly chaotic, it will be easier for him to get to and from work now. Gone are the days when, if there was a snarl-up in the traffic, Brian or any ex-pat for that matter, used to get out of their cars and direct the traffic until it had cleared. Nowadays you might get run over and such is the mood prevailing here at the moment that most expatriates now have Nigerian drivers so that they can leave them to sort their own problems out, and it is better if we just sit patiently, not getting involved, in the back of the car until the jam has cleared! Anyway, the house itself is really very nice, or will be when it has been painted throughout and brought up to scratch. Just off the main road on the Industrial estate are one or two cul-de-sacs where some quite large houses have been built in separate compounds. Our 'new' house is at the end of one of these cul-de-sacs, called Ashogbon Street. The road is only a dirt track really with huge pot holes appearing after the rains, which have obviously never properly been filled in, so just get larger and deeper and one has to drive very slowly and carefully in order to negotiate the huge holes. This is not easy in the dark as you can imagine, and as there are no lights on the road either, it can be quite tricky at times! The house is really a large bungalow on stilts, sounds odd I know but it is very practical and has an extremely spacious living area.

You drive through the gate into the compound, and park straight underneath the house. There is a large central store-cum-wash room which forms the central main pillar under the house and there are several slimmer pillars holding all the four corners of the house up which makes a large paved and shaded parking area for the cars underneath, and moreover, has plenty of room for the table tennis table!   A staircase goes up from the ground around three sides of the main pillar up to the front doors which are positioned centrally at the top.   There are two front doors, both with glass panels so that you can see exactly who is approaching from both sides of the house.   One door opens into the dining area and the other opens directly into the lounge area, which is really all the same room, but goes right through from the front of the house to the back.   Just off the dining end of the room is a kitchen which has a separate staircase down to the garden and the steward's quarters below, and on the other side is another room with sliding double doors where you can either sit in private and listen to music, which we will eventually set up in there, or else open the doors so that it becomes part of the main living area.   A door off the living-room leads to the three bedrooms which are also all quite large and airy.   Ours has an en-suite bathroom and one of the other bedrooms has an en-suite shower.   There is also a separate toilet for guests.   All the bedrooms have good double wardrobes which all need painting as they are heavily varnished in dark brown wood stain at the moment.   The windows all around the house are floor-to-ceiling, therefore letting in a maximum amount of light and there are enormous sliding glass windows both at the front and back of the main room, therefore when they are all opened up in the mornings you can benefit from any slightest breeze, which you can imagine, is very helpful in this heat.   All along the front of the house is a lovely wide balcony where you can sit and survey all that is going on in the garden below and beyond.   A lovely magenta-coloured bougainvillea climbs over the balcony in the front and is quite delightful to look at from the living room   We have just about cleared enough packing cases now to enable us to get into the rooms without having to climb all over them.

The painters started to paint before we moved in but they are so 'bush' I don't think they can have ever done it before. You won't believe this.   They have painted without rubbing anything down first and as they have painted without opening any windows or moving any of the curtains that had been left at the windows you can imagine the mess that greeted us! They have just sloshed it all on at the top of the windows in great globs and let it all run down to the bottom!   I don't think they speak any English as they just stared at me uncomprehendingly when I kept trying to explain how to do it.   Finally, they were driving me demented and I shouted at them so much in my frustration that they left and haven't returned so far.

Then came the 'electricians' who are driving me equally insane. Because we have no lights on this road, Brian insisted we had security lights put round the house. We do have iron grills covering some of the windows but not all of them, and it would be quite easy for somebody to shin over the wall into the compound at night without the night watchman being able to see them. The electricians have so far chipped long crooked grooves in the newly-painted outside walls and left their dirty finger marks all over the place when they were putting in the security lights. We have no power for much of every day at the moment so I'm not sure they will be very useful anyway. Maybe the power shortage is because we are on the industrial side of the town. The men have also had to make the holes larger in the walls where the air conditioners fit, because the ones we have bought across with us from the other house are larger than the old ones that were here. There are piles of plaster and cement dust in every room and huge holes in the walls now, letting in the mosquitoes, waiting until the plasterers can come and finish that job.

   The freezer that was here has packed up entirely and I managed to get a brand new one but that didn't seem to be working properly so any food that I could save is now distributed round Ikeja with friends. We asked the electrician to take the new freezer back to the factory for us in his van, for it to be checked out. When he delivered it back to us, we found that he had undertaken to mend it himself. He proudly showed off his handiwork to us and we were astounded to see that he had cut a six inch square hole in the outside enamel casing of the cabinet and *attached an electric fan to a meccano-like frame, which he explained would blow cold air into the inner workings of the freezer, and therefore would cool it down better! A few choice Anglo Saxon words from Brian told him in no uncertain terms just what he could do with it! Needless to say, when the power returns properly I shall now have to go and try to find yet another freezer.*

Next came the 'Tree people.' This compound has Casaurina trees all along the back and sides which have been left to grow too tall and therefore have become very thin and spindly. They can make quite a good looking hedge if tended to properly so we called some people in to cut them shorter along the top and sides so that they would eventually thicken up into a hedge. Well, so far we've had three bunches of idiots trying to do it. The first lot started to chop off all the branches and just left them looking like telegraph poles, so I sent them packing, the second lot had no ropes or anything and just hacked away at a 60ft. tree which they let fall right across the garden bringing down the telephone wire with it. That is no joke I can tell you, after being months and months without a phone, finally to get one that actually worked,--for less than a week! So they went with a flea in their ears as well. The third lot seem to be doing marginally better but the whole compound is like a jungle now and is full of cut trees and branches. The dust is unbelievable and together with all the Harmattan dust over the last two months it is decidedly intolerable.

Oh! Then we had the 'plumber!' This is classic. There is a very large sink in the store-room downstairs and it would be ideal for the steward to do the washing down there but for some unknown reason, there was no water connected and no taps on the sink. The plumber said he could easily run the water down from the kitchen direct to the sink below. He came to tell me when he had finished the job and I went down to admire his handiwork. Well, this 'handiwork', I noted, had consisted of hacking a great hole in the kitchen wall for the pipe to go through, that was big enough for me to climb through, as well as bashing up the existing taps on the sink in there in the process, taking the pipe down the outside wall, which meant that he had hacked a groove all the way down that, before knocking a big hole in the wall of the store-room below, to take the pipe through there and finally connect it to the sink and fix the new taps. After all that, when I turned the taps on the water ran out all over the floor and my feet! There was only a plug hole which was not connected to any outlet pipe! Honestly, you'd think he would have checked that wouldn't you? Then to cap it all, when we came to make dinner later that evening, we discovered that he had hacked his way through the gas pipe as well so we had no means of cooking either. At this point I went berserk! Everyone who has been to work on this house so far has just seemed to leave a trail of utter destruction.

The painters didn't return so I have resorted to painting the wardrobes and inside cupboards myself so

that at least I can get some kitchen stuff and clothes unpacked and put away. It isn't worth painting anything else at the moment anyway until all these so-called workmen have left the scene! It has been a bit like that old song of Flanders and Swann "T'was on a Monday morning when the Gas man came to call!"
A chapter of accidents all round so far.

We also took delivery of a brand new car last week. It is a Lancia Beta 2000 saloon. Brian and I went to pick it up in Lagos and it looked fantastic. By the time we got back to Ikeja, some 14 miles away, the gear mechanism had gone and we crawled the last few miles home with only a first and second gear!

To top all that, I heard some commotion going on in the compound the other day and went out on the balcony to see what was going on. Our gardener had lit some twigs and grass and was shoveling it into the middle of the wall which surrounds the compound. I shouted to him 'What are you doing?' 'Big snake Madame' came back the reply! I watched fascinated for a while but nothing was happening apart from the wall being set on fire! After a while, the gardener ran to connect the hose pipe to the water and eventually managed to put out the fire, whereupon this huge spitting cobra rose out of the wall, hood wide open, and dropped down at his feet writhing and thrashing around. I must say that the gardener Abel, and the steward were very brave and both set to and battered it into submission with spade and rake before finally finishing it off by chopping its head off with a machete!

After all that excitement, it's back to the mundane now, I need to get some curtains from our old house altered, so do you think you could send 22 yards of rufflette tape out with the children when they come for Easter please?

We have taken on a beautiful dog belonging to a couple from Pfizer who are leaving. He is part Boxer and part Ridgeback and his name is Tombo. He is settling down well and enjoys sitting out on the balcony watching all that goes on around him. The parrot isn't too keen on him yet and squawks loudly whenever he goes up to his cage for a sniff. He will be good for security though in this part of Ikeja. Brian is off to Accra again this week so I will be very glad to have Tombo here with me.

I'm afraid the children will need their cholera and smallpox jabs renewing before they come out again, so could you make sure they take their health cards to the school doctors and also could you please check in their passports to see if their re-entry permits are up to date? I think it is about a year since they were last done.

Must close now and hope that next week proves to be a bit better than this last one has been! Hope you and all the family are keeping well, we send all our love to you all of course

As Always,

Brian and Maureen.xxxx

CHAPTER 17 - NAIROBI 1978

I had enjoyed my trips to East Africa so much and even though Brian travelled there fairly often to the Pfizer office, he hadn't had much chance to see the game parks or any of the country outside of Nairobi. We had for a long time wanted to take the children to experience it for themselves and were so happy when the opportunity arose in December 1978 when we were all invited there, to spend Christmas with Pauline and Graham. We were so excited and couldn't wait to go. After Christmas, we planned to drive south to Mombasa and take in a few of the game parks on the way.

Livestock Feeds Ltd
PMB 1097
Ikeja
Lagos State

Jan. 1979

Dearest All,

Hope everybody is well and that you all enjoyed a wonderful Christmas.

I haven't had a minute to write letters until now but at last have plucked up the courage to write and tell you of our Christmas in Nairobi, and perhaps you will realise why I've been so long in writing to you all. I just couldn't face writing or even thinking about it again. Anyway, it is all over with now and I stress that we are all fine. The nerves are a bit shattered but apart from that we all seem to have handled the situation extremely well. We only hope that Nick won't worry too much about us being here now. He said to us one night, 'Dad do we have to live in Africa?' It's an experience that I'm afraid will be deeply etched on our minds for ever. People say 'time heals' and hopefully the awful memory will fade one day.

Firstly though, thank you all very much for the presents you sent out with the children. We took the smaller ones with us but I'm afraid we never got to open them as they were stolen in the debacle that I am about to relate.

We set off for the airport in Ikeja on the 22nd December at noon, so excited at the prospect of our holiday in Nairobi. When we got to the airport, we were told that our Pan Am flight was delayed. We didn't know it then but we were to sit for twelve hours, like cattle in a pen, having been checked in and gone through to the crowded departure lounge. Everyone was sweating in the intense heat. There were no drinks available, no air conditioning, and we were unable to open any windows as they were all sealed. The small departure lounge was totally packed with people, all trying to get their flights out of Nigeria in time for Christmas. Flight after flight was called and there was a near constant riot as people were trying to get through the painfully slow security check and out to their respective planes before they departed without them!

Our flight finally arrived, having had some technical trouble in Robertsfield on the way. It was not a very auspicious start! We finally got away at midnight. None of us slept on the flight and we arrived in Nairobi, exhausted, at 9 am local time, in the morning to be met by bright and smiling Graham and Pauline with their young son Robbie, who had all had a good long sleep the night before!

We had planned to do our Christmas shopping when we arrived in Nairobi as there was nothing to buy in the shops in Nigeria, so after lunch, we set off and managed to get a few bits and pieces. Unfortunately, some of the shops were shut by this time as the holidays had already started, so we decided to call it a day, and what we hadn't got, would have to wait until after Christmas.

That evening, we had been invited to a party by some friends who used to live in Nigeria and had fairly recently moved across to Nairobi.   We really felt too tired to go, but decided that we must at least put in an appearance as we might not have the opportunity to meet up with them again while we were there.   The children decided not to go and we promised them we would only stay there for an hour or two at most.   We had a lovely evening, meeting up with old friends and new, but -- Thank God we got home early.

Brian had not slept well for a few nights before we left, trying to sort out the business before the Christmas break, and then had not even dozed on the plane through the previous night.   He decided to take a couple of tranquilisers to ensure a good night's sleep. We were so tired after the journey and the stress of trying to leave Nigeria with all the chaos there, and it was such a relief when we finally fell into bed around midnight.

At about 2-15am, I was woken up by a strange noise, half shouting and half chanting, and the sound of feet jogging slowly past our window.   We were staying in a bungalow and had been warned by Pauline not to leave our bedroom window open more than a crack and certainly not to leave anything of value anywhere in sight, as the latest gossip was that robberies had recently been carried out in that area by the felons using a fishing rod and line with a large *hook on the end in order to hook valuables up from the other side of the room without there being any signs of a 'break-in'! My bed was directly under the window, so I sat up and peeped very carefully through the curtains.*

I saw several men jogging in a line past the window. They were all holding leafy branches in front of their faces. When the procession reached the 'Askari,' or night watchman, who was sitting on a chair outside the front door, they seemed to be going round and round his chair, still chanting. Graham and Pauline had also obviously heard something from their bedroom as the alarm and the security lights, which were operated by a switch situated by the side of their bed, suddenly came on. I saw a person talking to the night guard and although I couldn't understand what they were saying, it seemed to be fairly peaceful and I supposed, in my sleepy state, that it had to be some sort of Christmas ritual that was taking place between the locals. They then all hurried off round the other side of the house, leaving the askari on his chair and all was quiet again. Graham had switched off the alarm and the lights as he also thought it might have been a false alarm, and as they had an arrangement with their expatriate neighbours, who lived a short distance away in the next compound, that whenever the alarm sounded they would all come running, he didn't want to disturb people unnecessarily so near to Christmas. I lay down again thinking that they must have gone.

Within five minutes, there was an almighty crash of breaking glass, followed by the most horrendous banging and shouting and noise that I have ever heard. I leapt out of bed and had to shake Brian really hard to rouse him from his 'tranquillised' state. Graham was soon in the corridor outside our bedrooms, shouting for us all to get up as there were 'teefmen' in the house. I ran out into the corridor to get the children out of their bedrooms. They didn't know what the hell was going on and wondered what all the shouting and noise was about. Graham yelled for us all to go down to their bedroom which was at the far end of the corridor in the bedroom wing. Brian was completely naked and I was trying to find his pyjamas, but as I hadn't yet unpacked, I had no success, and in my panic to get the children down to the other bedroom, we just left everything and ran. By this time, the 'teefmen' were trying to break down the specially reinforced steel door to the bedroom wing. Graham was trying to fend them off with a piece of wood which they had by this time broken off the top of the door. The robbers were on the other side hacking at the door using iron bars and Pangas, which are like a Machete but with a long curved blade. The shouting, noise, banging, confusion and general panic was absolutely terrifying. Brian was trying to hold the door closed with Graham from our side but the wood started to splinter and we could see the blades of the pangas slicing through. I remember trying to find a golf club or something like that to give to Brian and

Graham but it wasn't long before the door crashed down and the gang rushed us all up the corridor, screaming and shouting wildly at us to get down on the floor. There must have been about eight of them and they peeled off into the various bedrooms, ranting and shouting and pulling open drawers and wardrobes, spilling all the contents onto the beds and floors. They wrenched off us and took all our watches and any jewellery that we were wearing. My mouth was totally dry and we were all shaking badly as I tried to squash down on the floor on top of Sally and Nick, between the bed and the wall, in an effort to hide them from these ghastly men. Pauline, to my utter astonishment, was on the phone, trying to get through to the police, but the robbers, thinking they had cut the telephone wires thought she was bluffing and shouted at her to get down on the floor as she wouldn't be able to get through to anyone. We later found out that they had indeed cut some telephone wires but they had mistakenly cut a neighbour's. Robbie was sitting on the bed with Pauline telling the robbers that we had nothing of any value in the house, and when they pulled out the drawers and were scattering the contents around, I remember him saying 'You see, it's all just 'tacky tacky.'

Meanwhile, we suddenly realised that Brian was not in the bedroom with us but had followed three of the robbers into the room where we had been sleeping. We heard sounds of fighting coming from down the corridor, and Graham, who was lying at the end of the bed, sat up and shouted "Brian, get back in

*here quickly' whereupon one of the robbers smacked
him straight across the chest and arm with his Panga.
Thank God it was with the flat of the blade, otherwise
he would have been sliced in half.   Pauline had
managed to switch the alarm and lights back on and
this incensed the robbers even further as they started
shouting at her to switch them off.   I remember
looking up to see one of them who had a green woolly
hat on his head, his eyes were wide and staring hard at
us and he was obviously high on drugs.   I was terrified
we were all going to be raped.   The Africans were
always fascinated by Sally's long blonde hair and liked
to stroke it and feel the soft silkiness which was so
unlike their own.   I was petrified that he was just
about to grab her, when all of a sudden there was the
sound of gunfire outside.   This time, I thought our
end had really come but amazingly, the robbers took to
their heels and ran with whatever they were carrying
in their arms.*

*Graham jumped up and chased through the
lounge where the once beautifully polished parquet
floor was now covered with broken glass from the large
patio windows that they had heaved a huge rock
through so that they could break in.   Graham lifted
this rock and in a complete fury threw it after them as
they disappeared down the garden and away into the
night. Several days later, Brian and Graham tried to
lift the same rock again to move it back to it's proper
place in the garden, but found they could hardly lift it
between them.   Sheer adrenaline had given him the*

strength that night. Meanwhile, we all sat up, trembling and shaking and feeling lucky to be alive, when Graham brought Brian back into the bedroom and said "For God's sake Maureen, do something with Brian's back!'

Brian had blood streaming down his face and I jumped up, shocked, to help him, but as he turned round to go into the bathroom, I couldn't believe what I saw. His back, across his shoulder had a wide gaping wound from which the blood was pumping out and running all down his back. We quickly got him to the bath where he sat on the edge while I grabbed the nearest towel and tried to staunch the bleeding. While I tried to draw the wound together and also the one on his forehead, much of what followed is still rather a blur. I remember that Brian was asking for a cigarette and we were all saying, no that he shouldn't smoke in case he had to have an anaesthetic or something, but Brian just kept saying give me a cigarette please, until little Robbie piped up. 'For goodness sake, just give him a cigarette!' Graham suddenly realised that his feet were cut and bleeding from the glass that had gone into them when he chased across the lounge floor. The next stupid thing I remember was trying to get Brian into a pair of Graham's old trousers so that we could get him to the hospital with some clothes on! Brian was very slim in those days but still rather larger than Graham, so there was no way we could get them on him. I finally found some of his own in our suitcase. Then, their very kind neighbour, Jim arrived at the door, having

239

driven down in his car.   They had heard the alarms and, as promised, had run to get the policeman who was guarding his neighbour's house at the top of the hill because he had a rifle, and had then come down to see what it was all about.   It had been his neighbour's guard who had fired the shot that had frightened the robbers off the premises.   Jim's neighbour, mercifully for us, just happened to be the Minister of Finance for Kenya, therefore had a properly trained and armed guard at his house both day and night.

Jim quickly bundled Graham into the front seat and Brian and I into the back where I was still trying to hold together the gaping wound on his back, with the wet towels.   We set off for the hospital in Nairobi.   As we drove up the long driveway to the road at the top, I remember seeing Pauline leading the children up the driveway to Jim's house where his wife was waiting for them.   Nick had a terrible attack of asthma as a result of the shock and the stress of it all. I was desperate to be with the children to comfort them but we had to get to hospital quickly and Pauline assured me they would be alright with her.   We were all still in a terrible state of shock but lucky to be alive.

It took us about half an hour to get to the hospital, I remember getting out of the car still trying to hold on to Brian's back and only when a kind Doctor led him away, did I realise that I was still in my night dress which was by this time covered in blood. The Doctor and nurses were concerned that I had also been cut but pleased when I assured them it was

Brian's blood and not from me.   I had to sit in the waiting room in this state, while Brian and Graham were being treated for their various cuts and bruises.   I was still shaking so much from shock and felt very cold too by then, so Jim finally said he would take me back to see how Pauline and the children were and to get some warm clothes on.   When we got there, Pauline said the children had stayed up at Jim's house and seemed to have settled for the night.   She didn't want to bring them down to see the house again in the state it was in.   It looked as if there had been a massacre as there was blood all over the walls and down the corridor.   Pauline was valiantly trying to sweep up the glass and put things back into drawers and wardrobes. She told us that the police had been and that the Askari had been found tied to his chair with barbed wire!   This was obviously what they were doing to him when I saw them going round and round his chair before they broke into the house!

Jim took me back to the hospital after I had showered and changed and I seem to remember that dawn had broken long before we were allowed home that day.   Brian had suffered some severe shock and vomiting after the anaesthetic.   He had been stitched up and they wanted to keep him sedated for a while to check that he was alright.   The young Kenyan Doctor was very good and had put five stitches in his forehead where Brian remembered later, he had been hit with a sort of truncheon that had a nail protruding from the end, which easily could have gouged his eye out.   He had managed to wrestle the truncheon off him and hit *his assailant across the head with it. The Panga wound across his back had cut through the muscle in his shoulder and so he had several internal stitches before he had thirteen external ones across his back. The Doctor said he was very lucky that there didn't seem to have been any other damage to the lungs or nerve endings. Graham had many glass splinters painstakingly taken out of his feet, and the following day he had a mighty bruise across his chest and arm in the shape of the Panga blade.*

Graham had to organise someone to come and board the windows up to make the place secure. This was not an easy task on Christmas Eve I might add but he managed to get someone from the office to organise it. The police came round and had to take our finger-prints and hear all the evidence. Brian was still sedated and feeling very groggy. We had to try to assess what had been stolen. Quite a lot of our stuff had been taken because it was still in the suitcases which hadn't really been unpacked and they had grabbed one of those. It was when Brian had gone into the bedroom after the robbers, that he had discovered them picking up our passports and he had said to them' Don't take those please, they are no earthly use to you' when one of the robbers hit him over the head with the truncheon that he was holding. Brian wrested an iron bar away from him, as all he had picked up to defend himself with until then was a hairbrush and he hit the robber back over the head with the bar. The robber went down but unfortunately, he hadn't hit him hard enough and as Brian was confronting the other one, the first one got up again and slashed Brian's back open with his Panga.

Graham decided that we would all feel more secure if we moved into the Serena Hotel in the centre of Nairobi for the rest of the holiday as the house was in such a shambles. Pauline had previously made many of the preparations for Christmas though, and so we all decided that we would sleep at the hotel and come back to the house during the day and try to carry on as normally as possible. We were determined that our Christmas was not going to be spoiled, so after the fingerprints had been taken, we tried to clean up the house as much as we could and get on with the rest of the preparations for Christmas Day.

Brian was still heavily sedated and very badly bruised and sore so spent most of Christmas Eve in bed. We were invited to the kind neighbours for drinks before lunch and while we were there, the senior police inspector called at Graham's house in person and roused Brian to tell him that they thought they had caught five of the men who had broken in the previous night. He wanted us all to go to the station and identify them. Brian said we would go when the rest of us returned home. When we got back a short time later and Brian told Graham what the Police officer had said, Graham was reticent to comply. He pointed out to us that if the police had only found five of the men, there were still several 'at large.' If we identified any, or all of the men that they were holding, then it would mean that these men would probably be lined

243

up and shot, as this was the punishment they meted out in Kenya. Graham was very worried that as he and his family still had to live there, there may be some retribution against them from the others who were involved and still 'at large.' He was, therefore, very reluctant to identify only a few of the perpetrators. We agreed that until they found the rest of the 'gang,' we would not go to identify those that were being held.

Christmas Day was a triumph for us all. We arrived at the house early from the hotel, and ignoring the boarded up windows and blood smeared walls, we had a lovely traditional lunch of roast turkey with all the trimmings, followed by Christmas pudding and brandy sauce. We played traditional Christmas music and toasted all our families back home. If we had to be in that situation with anybody, then Graham, Pauline and Robbie were our very best companions to have, as they always kept up a fantastic sense of humour and wit at all times. Brian was feeling very stiff and sore and sporting a beautiful black eye, which throughout the next week, turned all the colours of the rainbow!

The children were fantastic. We had no hysterics from anyone and they tried, along with us, to turn Christmas into a fun occasion. Nick had a very bad bout of asthma and so was feeling pretty lousy but tried not to show it. We had unfortunately lost a lot of our stuff as the robbers had taken, among other things, my hand luggage which contained all my jewellery, three cameras, Christmas presents, make-up, etc. They had also taken Sally's handbag which contained her passport and jewelery and make-up. Other items of clothing, duty-free cigarettes, jeans and stuff they had grabbed on their way out were also missing. Brian had managed to hold on to our passports and travellers cheques together with my hairbrush which was the one he had tried to use as a weapon! We had survived pretty much intact, for which we were all very thankful. It could have been so much worse.

On Boxing Day Pauline and Graham had arranged an 'open house' and we decided to carry on with it. We were still sleeping at the hotel but going back to the house during the day. News had spread like wildfire of course so everyone came to offer their condolences and try to 'jolly' things up for us. I remember talking to one of Graham's Kenyan colleagues, who was adamant that the robbers would not have been Kenyans but had probably crossed over the border from Uganda as they were the 'bad people.' He showed us what we should have done as they were breaking the door down and we were absolutely horrified as he demonstrated in front of everyone present with a canister of fly spray that he got from the kitchen. After shaking it vigorously he took the top off and simultaneously sprayed and lit the vapour with his cigarette lighter, whereupon an enormous flame shot out from the end of the canister. " It would have burned their eyes out' he said laughingly "and they would soon have run away!' We had to arrange to renew Sally's passport with the British High Commission the next day and we also found the

Nigerian Embassy were very co-operative about putting a re-entry Visa into the new passport as soon as it was ready. Usually these things take months to arrange.

The following day, we set off to drive down to the coast for a couple of days' relaxation. The drive took seven hours and we set off early, making a stop at 'Hunters Lodge' for breakfast on the way. The scenery was vast and interesting all the way down to Mombasa. We stayed at a brand new hotel which was right on the beach called the Africana Lodge Hotel. The bedrooms were individual Rondavel huts built of wood and thatch but each with an airy bedroom and bathroom. Mombasa has a very humid climate so we were grateful to have air conditioning in the rooms.

We really enjoyed being able to relax on the beach and Robbie and Nick went para-gliding which was very exciting for them. It wasn't the normal method of Para-gliding though. The boys were put in a special harness which was attached to a tractor, which then set off at a fast pace down the beach and when the wind filled the parachute contraption that was attached to the harness, it lifted the boys into the air. The only trouble was that Nick was quite light and thin and so he stayed up there until the tractor had to go into reverse to get him down again when they had reached the end of the beach! Poor Nick was still feeling pretty lousy and we had started him on antibiotics by then so both he and Brian were having to stay in the shade for most of the time. We tried to catch up on sleep but the power went off and there was no air conditioning on our second night! Ah! Africa! We thought it only happened in Nigeria! The electricity company of Nigeria is known as NEPA which stands for National Electrical Power Authority but to all the expatriate community it is translated and referred to as' Never Eny Power Anywhere!'

On the way back a couple of days later, we stopped off in Tsavo West Game Park and saw elephant, zebras, giraffe and even lion this time, which I was very thrilled about as I had never seen them in the wild before. It was very exciting for the children to see them on their first time in a big game park too. We also visited Mzima Springs and saw the hippos and crocodile lazing at the side of the pool. We arrived back at the Serena Hotel in Nairobi later that evening and had the first good night's sleep we had had for over a week. None of us had admitted it before, but I think all of us had been suffering 'flashbacks' from the stress of the attack.

On New Year's Eve, we packed up a pic-nic and drove to the rift valley to Lake Naivasha for the day. Robbie and Nick were keen to hire a boat and row out on the lake. Unfortunately, it was the time of year when the lake becomes full of weeds near the shore, so they found it very difficult to move, let alone to row anywhere. It kept them occupied for an hour or so before they eventually admitted defeat and gave up! We had hoped to see millions of flamingo and pelicans on the lake, but these were sadly depleted at this time and so we only saw very few. They are beautiful birds though, particularly in flight, and we hoped that they had only migrated to Lake Nakuru because of the water weeds that had grown over the surface of Lake Naivasha at this time of year.

That evening we had been invited to another party in Nairobi but we decided against it and preferred instead to have a quiet dinner in a local Italian restaurant and then go back to the Hotel room and let the New Year in together. We were just on the way up to our room with a few bottles of wine when we realised that we didn't have a cork screw. By the time we finally managed to get one from a member of staff at the hotel, we happened to be in the lift when the clock struck midnight! So we all had another rather unusual New Year Celebration in 1978, in a lift! Well, at least we were on the way up! We all made a wish that it would stay that way for the rest of the year.

Brian, Sally, Nick and I set off very early the next morning to drive up to the Abadare Mountains in the Nyandarua National Park. We arrived at the Country Club in time for a superb lunch after having missed our turning and driven on for several miles further than we should have. It was only when we passed the sign saying that we were on the Equator that we realised our mistake. It was actually quite amazing to stop and take photos of ourselves next to the sign of the Equator and although it was incredibly hot in the sunshine, to look up and see Mt. Kenya not far away, and see that it was covered in snow.

During the lunch, we were entertained by some of the local tribesmen, who in truth, looked quite scary, all dressed in their loin cloths and head dresses and covered with white and black markings, which were painted over their entire bodies and faces. They did a frenzied war dance to the loud sounds of the rapidly beating drums, together with much posturing and threatening gestures towards all the guests, with their spears and shields. Although it was entertaining for most of the other guests, I wasn't too sure we were ready for that after what we had just been through.

After lunch, together with the other tourists who were staying, we were trundled off in a couple of clapped-out old buses to drive to a place called 'The Ark.' This is a relatively new luxury hunting lodge built in the Abadare Forest. It is built on stilts, of wooden construction which is designed to look and feel as if one is really on Noah's Ark. We had to alight from the buses and carrying our luggage, walk across a narrow, roughly constructed, wooden bridge, at tree top height, and into the Lodge. Our rooms were rather like log cabins but with windows which faced the water hole for optimal viewing of all the animals. We were lucky to see a leopard almost immediately we arrived there. He slunk out of the bushes in front of us, stalked by a hyena and into a clearing beyond. Unconcerned, they both stopped for about five minutes in the clearing, which allowed all the visitors to get busy with their cameras before the animals continued on their way. We had borrowed a camera from Graham as ours had been stolen in the robbery but it

249

was very difficult to get good pictures in the wild, and as we were not used to the camera and the camouflage of the animals against the backdrop of bushes, grasses and shadows, we didn't manage to acquire many clear pictures on that trip. An enormous variety of animals came into the water hole that afternoon and throughout the night. We were all quite transfixed watching them and extremely lucky to have seen so many, especially as there has been so much rain this season and the animals had no real reason to come into the watering holes as it is already quite lush throughout the 'bush.' It is incredible how close we were able to get to the animals as they were right below us, so people could only speak in whispers and had to stay very still. Apart from elephant, we saw rhino, buffalo, hyena, various varieties of deer, genet cats, mongoose, wart hogs, and giant forest hogs, colobus monkeys, and very many different species of birds.

At around midnight, we were rewarded with the sight of one of the most rare animals of the forest, the bongo. This is a beautiful species of antelope with lovely striped markings on his soft brown coat. They are very shy, timid creatures and rarely seen. If requested to do so, the lodge alerts people who have already gone to bed, by sounding a small alarm in their rooms to tell the occupants that the species they have asked to see is at the water hole. We were still up and viewing, when other guests who had retired to bed, came hurrying back to the lounge as quickly and quietly as possible to see this rare sight. Apparently another 21 Bongo came in for a drink during that night, but we were happy to have seen one and so went off to bed very satisfied, even though it becomes very difficult to tear oneself away. Sadly, we had to leave that magical place at sunrise the next morning and drive back to Nairobi as we only had two more days of our holiday left before returning to Nigeria.

In the afternoon, we had arranged to pick up Sally's new passport, only to be told that her old one had been found in the grounds of St. Austin's Church. We drove over to pick it up from the Catholic Father who had found it. The health cards were missing and it did have blood stains on some of the pages. Fortunately, one of the Doctors at Pfizer wrote out some new cards for her and these were signed and verified by a contact that Graham had at the airport so at least Sally didn't have to go through the misery of having all the injections for yellow fever, typhoid and paratyphoid again, which can be extremely painful and debilitating.

Another treat we had before leaving Nairobi was going to a drive-in movie that night. Never having been to one before we found it quite fun. We had to be in two cars of course but parked next to the Penfolds, we were able to pass beer and cokes back and forth whilst having hamburger and chips at the same time as watching the movie. Quite a novelty!

Our arrival back in Nigeria wasn't too good either as our driver didn't turn up to meet us and so we had to fight along with the masses to try to get a taxi home. Brian learnt the next day that after we *had left for Nairobi before Christmas, our driver had been asked to take another Pfizer expatriate family to the airport a couple of days later. He used our car and after dropping them off at the airport, had apparently decided to use it for himself. He went off to a bar somewhere, got drunk and crashed the car on his way home. He was still languishing in the local jail when we returned. His family came to Brian begging him to pay money so they could get him out. Brian decided to let him cool his heels in jail for a little while longer!*

Well, it's nearly time for the children to go back to school again. Always a sad time for us all. Their flights are booked for the 12th as you know but still only on a waiting list so we really hope they manage to get on the same one together. We won't be able to let you know though so we just hope that it all works out for you and that you don't have to have any unnecessary trips back and forth to the airport and schools, etc. We do so appreciate all you do for us and we really hope you understand how difficult it is for us from this end. Please let us know soonest that they have arrived safely.

Our love to you all, as always and our thanks again for all the lovely things you sent out for us at Christmas, even though, as I said, sadly, we never even got to see some of them as they were stolen in the robbery. I will write again soon, As always,

Maureen and Brian xxxx

CHAPTER 18 - A TIME OF CHANGE

Writing that letter home brought all the horror back to me and we began to realise in the ensuing months that it had affected us all quite badly. Brian shut it out of his mind completely and wouldn't recall any of that awful night for many years. Things were getting quite difficult in Nigeria too. We had always put up with power and water shortages, no telephones and very little food or commodities in the shops. There were many more robberies taking place in homes and on the highways now and expatriates seemed to be the main targets. In the past, we had almost felt sorry for the people who robbed our houses as there was usually a spate of them just before Christmas or term time began, when the Nigerians had to pay for uniforms and books to enable them to send their children to school. They usually stole our stereo equipment, clothes, shoes and jewellery, or anything that they could sell in the market place. Often we suspected it was an 'inside job,' as the robbers seemed to know when we would be out and the house empty. Normally the staff excuses were that they were either in their quarters in the compound or the night watch had gone off sick and so we could never prove anything. One night we were fast asleep in bed when we were robbed of some of our clothes from wardrobes in our bedroom, watches from the bedside tables, and even jewellery from the dressing-table drawers and we never heard a thing. I am a very light sleeper and normally was wide awake at the slightest noise or movement, but we only discovered it in the morning, when Brian found a pair of his trousers and a cuff link box which had been dropped half way down the corridor! This made us think that we had been drugged somehow as not even the dog had barked! Another time, we arrived back from the beach one Sunday afternoon to find that the house had been broken into again, this time through the front door and when questioned, the staff all said they 'hadn't seen or heard anything!' The stereo equipment had gone again! We always thought that as long as they didn't harm us, then it was OK. as we could usually replace stereo equipment, less so the jewelery of course, and over time, I lost most of mine to thieves so had decided never to have any good stuff out in Nigeria with me again. Normally, when husbands were away on tour, or out of the country, friends always invited the wives to dinner in the evenings and usually I had been happy to drive home myself and stay on my own in the house at night, as we always had a dog; now though, friends insisted I stay the night with them and likewise, we did the same for the wives of our friends who were away on business.

In February 1976 Brigadier Murtala Mohammed was assassinated. This was the coup that had taken place while we were at the Trade Fair in Ghana, when his car had been ambushed while he was on the way to his office in Lagos. He was succeeded by his Chief of Staff Olesegun Obasanjo who subsequently completed the plan which had been set into place by Mohammed who had vowed to hand over power to Civilian rule as soon as possible. Obasanjo handed over the Presidency to Shehu Shagari, a civilian politician, on October 1st 1979. Murtala Mohammed became a National hero even though he had only been in power for seven months, and the new airport in Ikeja was subsequently named after him. Brian came to know Obasanjo after he had handed over the Presidency to Shagari and had then bought a poultry farm to occupy him in his retirement. He bought his supplies from Livestock Feeds of course! Obasanjo was re-elected as President in 2003 and served until 2007.

Meanwhile, as part of the indigenisation programme Brian had been training his Nigerian assistant to be managing director of Livestock feeds Nigeria whilst himself moving into his new position as Director of Agricultural Development Pfizer West Africa. The large corporate companies who had once employed expatriate management and housed whole expatriate families were all now having to employ Nigerians as the top managers. Many of our friends were leaving and having to move on to various positions in other parts of the world. Renting houses in Nigeria became an enormous expense for the companies because landlords started to charge the full rent up to five years in advance, which enabled them to build another house to be rented out at exorbitant rates. Greed became an obsession! Gradually, it became more economical for companies to send executives and engineers out to work in Nigeria on a more frequent but temporary basis for two or three months at a time, rather than house them and their families full time in Nigeria. In the larger companies, one house might have been kept on as a guest house for visiting personnel or if they worked in Lagos, apartments that were being built on Victoria Island were becoming a more popular option for companies to rent.

Brian was working on developing the franchise operations in West and North Africa, travelling to Cairo, Nairobi and the States and also working on a massive project to build a facility at the new port, called Tin Can Island, which was in the development stages in Apapa, near Lagos, that would be able to handle deliveries of grain in bulk and at the same time export the finished products made by Livestock Feeds to any other African country. After the booming economy, Nigeria began to realise that they couldn't exist entirely on imported goods and that it was necessary to produce their own essential commodities. The oil wasn't going to last forever! Lack of telephones, water shortages and power cuts were still a huge problem. This also created major difficulties for businesses and the traffic jams increased fourfold as it meant that you had to drive to Lagos and back in order to speak to anyone there, or fly to other parts of the country to enable you to conduct business in other regions. It was almost impossible at one time in 1978 to buy beer or soft drinks and then they banned imported meat hoping to encourage more meat production in Nigeria. It was almost like it had been just after the Biafran war. It just wasn't possible to meet the needs of the Nigerian people let alone the expatriate community as they were banning imports before they had set up the means of producing their own. Regarding the traffic jams, the 'classic' solution they came up with that would help relieve the congestion was that only vehicles with odd registration numbers could travel on Mondays, Wednesdays and Fridays and only vehicles with even numbers could travel on Tuesdays, Thursdays and Saturdays! What happened in reality was that many people got two cars, one with odd and one with even number registrations on, so the problem didn't improve! It actually got worse! Rumour had it that the less scrupulous had two sets of registration plates, and yes, you've guessed it, one set ending with an odd number and the other ending with an even one! It was rather like the time when the Nigerian Government decided to change from driving on the left hand side of the road to driving on the right. Nobody ever really understood why this should be necessary, however, there was supposed to be a curfew on the night before the change over and no one was to be allowed on the road after six o'clock in the evening on the date in question until six o'clock the following morning, when everyone was then supposed to change over and drive on the right. Not everyone got that message and we even heard that someone had announced on some of the local radio stations that the lorries were going to change over on one day and the cars on the next! In the event, that didn't happen but when the change-over did take place, even more chaos reigned on all the roads.

Rumours began to circulate that as Lagos had just about reached saturation point, a new Capital City was going to be built and that it would probably be situated to the north of Lagos and approximately in the centre of the country. This meant that new roads and rail links would also have to be developed and built, together with Government offices, hospitals, schools and office buildings, hotels and houses, etc., and a whole new city would spring up in an area that was at that time only inhabited by a few indigenous people who lived in mud houses and scratched a living from the soil. Could this be possible? Judging by the state of the country at that moment, nobody really believed that it would ever happen!

Brian was doing quite a fair amount of travelling and many of the companies were now giving their expatriate staff five month tours in Nigeria followed by a couple of weeks back in the UK to alleviate the stress levels. It was becoming quite difficult for companies to function properly at that time and also, because our children were growing up fast and facing A-levels and GCE exams at school I really wanted to be in England to support them. We had a house in Walton on Thames which we had been renting out but decided that now was the time to take it over permanently ourselves and make it more of a base for all of us. It was handily situated near the station and between Heathrow and Gatwick airports and so was accessible for all of us, not to mention to many of our friends and family who happened to be passing through! For the next couple of years Brian managed to get home twice during the summer months so that meant that I could go back to UK at the beginning of June and stay until the middle of September, and was therefore able to attend Sports days and Speech days, parent teacher evenings, half-terms and holidays, on a more regular basis, which was lovely for me.

Unfortunately Pfizer were becoming increasingly reticent about expanding their Agricultural facility in Nigeria. Since Brian had been forced to hand over to a Nigerian manager, and it was becoming even more difficult to import goods into the country, they were dithering about building the facility in the new docks in Apapa or doing anything about the pig and poultry breeding project he was working on in Cairo. They were happy to let Brian carry on in Nigeria as they didn't want to lose him but as they had no other Agricultural business anywhere in the world, other than the Vet-Agriculture business they had in Nairobi, they had nothing else to offer him. Brian began to get very disheartened. He also had to sit and watch as the Livestock Feeds business that he had built up to a multi-million pound success story for Pfizer, slowly began to unravel and he also began to suspect that a good deal of the profit was going into some of the new management's back pockets rather than back into the business! The franchise managers he had set up around the country and in Ghana all wanted to continue to work with Brian and when a company from the UK, who also traded with Nigeria in a small way, said that they would back him, plus a Chief in Lagos who was also a respected Judge, encouraged him to form another company to import grain and manufacture animal feeds, Brian went ahead with his plans.

In 1980, he tendered his resignation to Pfizer and with great regret on all sides, we packed our personal belongings and left them and our dog with a friend, before we were given a suitable send-off by the company and many 'farewell' parties by friends. Brian then set up the new company which he called Agri Products and began to 'commute' to and from Nigeria for several months at a time, staying with friends whenever he could as we no longer had a house there. There were several set backs as it proved extremely difficult to do anything at all in Nigeria without enormous hassle or stumbling blocks in the way. Finally when work permits and visas were sorted out and it looked as if the business was at last about to go ahead, Brian thought the time had come for me to go out and start organising somewhere for us to live. We still had very dear friends in the Pfizer Pharmaceutical side who had a company house out there, but Jean was about to go back to the States as she was expecting a baby and husband Mike was going to be there on his own for a while before he too left Nigeria as they had been posted to Nairobi. They said we could use their house until it was time for them to pack up and go. I went out to join Brian at the beginning of March just in time to see Jean before she went off to the States. I was really happy to be back again after a long, cold and wet winter in England. We arranged for Sally and Nick to come out and join us for their Easter holidays and were all excited at the prospect of being back in Ikeja again.

Agri-Products Ltd.
P.O. Box 554
Ikeja
LAGOS STATE
Nigeria

April 1981

Dearest All,

Just to let you know that Sally and Nick both arrived safely. What a panic about Nick's ticket, but thank you so much for sorting it all out and picking him up from school and then running him to the airport at such last minute notice.

As you know, we are staying at Mike and Jean's house at the moment but Mike was away for the first week I was here and Jean has gone back to the States to have her baby. The house is rather infested with ants and cockroaches and badly needs fumigating but with Mike leaving shortly he obviously isn't going to do anything about getting it sprayed at this stage. We are just thankful to have a roof over our heads until we can sort one out for ourselves. Talking about having a roof over our heads reminds me that we very nearly didn't last week. Brian got a repeat bout of malaria and so retired early to bed with a raging fever. During the night a fantastic storm blew up when the wind was at gale force and the rain fell down in torrents. It sounded as if someone had turned a high pressure hose full on to the windows and was throwing gravel onto the corrugated iron roof. About five minutes later, the rain started pouring in through the ceiling right onto our bed. We leapt up and tried to move the bed but within minutes it was cascading in like a waterfall and we were getting soaked. Nick suddenly dashed in as the same thing was happening in his room. The power had gone off and we couldn't see what was going on but by this time we were wading around in about three inches of water and I had to get Brian out of there as he still had a fever. We banged on Sally's door to get her up, as we all sleep with doors locked here, and she was sleeping in Mike's bed while he was away. Fortunately his room was fairly dry, with water only trickling down the wall in one place. We got Brian into that bed, found a torch and splashed back to see if we could save anything. By this time, water was pouring in through all the fitted cupboards, soaking our clothes, sheets, blankets, towels and everything that was stored in them. We decided that there was absolutely nothing that we could do that night, so we all piled into Mike's bed with Brian, plus their Alsatian dog Kanga, who was positively shaking and terrified of the storm. Fortunately, it was a king-size bed, but even so, we all spent a few rather uncomfortable hours as you can imagine, and I was the one that ended up sleeping at the bottom!

The next morning, this place looked like a Chinese laundry! All the carpets, clothes, shoes, sheets, blankets, etc., had to be hung outside from every available bush, tree, wall, or patch of grass that we could find. We strung extra lines across the garden to try and dry everything out. I even had to go out and buy another iron so that I could help the steward to iron all the stuff when it was dry because anything that is hung outside here has to be ironed in order to kill the dreaded tumble fly who lay their eggs in the clothing. If they are not ironed, the eggs eventually burrow into one's skin and the grubs, which look like maggots, then grow inside you until they are big enough to hatch out. They look and feel like boils until this happens and then leave a big crater in the flesh after they go.

In spite of all the water falling from the sky, we don't have any coming through the mains here and so are having it delivered by a tanker three times a week. Goodness knows where it is coming from because it is all dark brown. Don't worry, we boil and filter any water that we drink or use for cooking, but the clothes and ourselves don't look or feel very clean after washing!

To say thank you and farewell to Mike, we had organised a huge party for him on the Saturday night after he returned. Sixty odd-people had been invited so a great deal had to be organised. Beer and drinks had to be ordered, collected and cooled, so we had to buy another fridge and borrow a cooler. Nick suggested a barbecue would be the best for so many people as we couldn't possibly cook everything in the kitchen here, or accommodate that many inside the

house.   We also had to beg and borrow another
barbecue, plates, cutlery, glasses, another bar, ice
buckets, cold boxes and ice, and as much beer as
friends could spare as it is very scarce here at the
moment.   Finally it was all organised and we worked
solidly for a couple of days beforehand, preparing food
and fetching and carrying all the stuff we were
borrowing, including a pick-up truck, which enabled us
to move it all. That afternoon, we collected small tables
and chairs from the golf club and set them up all
around the garden.   Sally and I meticulously taped
paper over the tops of the old tables we had borrowed
and then covered them with cloths, arranged little
bowls of flower arrangements made from frangipani
blossoms on every table, had candles and native lights
twinkling in the grass; these are made from old
evaporated milk cans that we fill with kerosene and a
wick, they smell horrible but look quite attractive! We
lit the mosquito coils which were smouldering under
the tables in order to prevent the guests being bitten.
Everything was just about ready.   Brian and Mike lit
the barbecues and then rushed off to the golf club to
have a shower so that we could preserve what water we
had left here for the toilets.

          The first guests began to arrive and things were
just getting under way when wham bam, the wind
suddenly blew up out of nowhere!   We were about to
have a line-storm! When the wind arrives like that,
you have about three minutes to get everything inside
before the rain comes. We just couldn't believe it! The
night-watches were scurrying about trying to catch

tablecloths and candles that were blowing away into the night, the chickens had already been put on the barbecues to cook, what a nightmare it was turning out to be! Suddenly, I thought about the bedrooms, as the roof hadn't yet been repaired! The guests that were already here, ran to help us move the beds, pull everything out of the wardrobes and cupboards again and pile them all in the driest part of the house, then the rain hit us again. The rest of the guests who were just arriving got absolutely drenched, splashing across the garden and into the house in the torrential rain that was pouring once again out of the sky. In the end, it turned out to be a really fun night. Of course there is great excitement when it rains here anyway, and it isn't cold rain and doesn't last long usually so people don't mind getting wet as it soon gets steamy and dry again when it stops. We put corrugated iron sheets (from the roof) over the barbecues and so they kept alight, we had plenty to drink for the guests, who were all beginning to get slightly blotto by then, and having a jolly good time. After about two hours the storm was over and everyone helped to set it all up outside again, albeit without the flowers and candle lights, but nevertheless, all in a very merry mood. We didn't eat until quite late of course and the last guests finally left at four in the morning with everyone declaring it had been a really fun evening! Sunday was spent clearing up and returning all the borrowed stuff back from whence it came. Poor Brian had to stay in bed again on Monday morning as he had got up far too soon after his bout of Malaria and consequently the fever had returned.

Mike finally left here on Thursday (having heard that Jean had given birth to their baby daughter on the night of our party would you believe). He had arranged for the packers to come in to move all their stuff but hadn't had the time to pack anything himself, and so I was left sorting out all Jean's clothes, their furniture and household goods, that were being shipped to Nairobi. Being American of course, they had been allowed to bring most of their personal and household belongings with them including their own beds. This meant that we had nothing for us to sleep on until some kind friends sent a couple of spare mattresses round for us to use on the floor!

On the Saturday morning, which was Easter, the packers were due to finish off and clear all the boxes out of the way. I got up early and leaving the family asleep went off to the shops as it was a holiday weekend, and we had little or no food left in the house. I was delighted to find some imported lamb and bacon in Kingsway. The price was exorbitant but I bought some anyway, and after finishing the rest of my shopping started back home. I had just turned into the driveway at the house and before the day watch could get the gate closed, another car followed me in and stopped right behind me. I thought it must have been a friend that I had just passed and waved to on the road who had turned round and followed me back to talk to me. I got out of the car and as I turned to greet her, saw that it was two Nigerian men who were *rushing towards me shouting loudly and one was cocking a gun in a frenzy. I couldn't think what was happening for a second or two until I realised that this was a robbery and they were wanting to steal the car and maybe shoot me!*

Suddenly I remembered my shopping was in the boot, and knowing just how difficult it was to get imported meat, I was furious and stamping my foot, said 'I'll just get my shopping out of the boot!' whereupon their frenzy and shouting became even more urgent, and I realised that they wouldn't hesitate to shoot me if I didn't hand over the keys. I stepped back and saw Brian running down the drive with a golf club in his hand ready to attack them so I called to him to stay where he was as they had guns. The robbers jumped in our car, which was brand new by the way and together with another guy who was driving their car, quickly reversed both cars out of the drive, leaving us to watch helplessly as they sped away. It had all happened so quickly that the steward and the packers who were busy in the house hadn't even noticed the commotion. The 'day watch' who was as terrified as I was and frozen in fear had done nothing. I later found out that Nick had been watching through a window but had been hanging onto the dog Kanga, fearing that if he had let him go and he had attacked the robbers they would have shot us all. Thankfully, no one was hurt but I was initially mostly angry about losing the car and my shopping until I got into the house and then I just sat and shook violently as the shock set in.

A kind neighbour took Brian up to the nearest police station to report the theft but after all the form-filling that he had to do it was well over an hour before the officer reported it, over a rather archaic radio, to any of the other stations. The car would have been well away and probably over the border by then. This is happening so often nowadays and there are loads of police checks and patrols out everywhere but they only seem to be causing more delays and disruption to the traffic than positively helping to catch any of the robbers. With all the procedures and hassle that you have to go through when reporting a theft no one ever seems to get caught because the system all takes far too long. Brian had to go again to the police station that night and then I had to go the following morning to give a statement and as there were two different officers dealing with the case, that pretty much tells us that it will never be found!

We have to move out of this house next week and some old friends who have just returned to Nigeria after being away for about six years have kindly said we can move in with them until we find something for ourselves. We are not having much luck at the moment as the prices have rocketed up and landlords are presently demanding rent payable for five years in advance! A new car is going to cost us upwards of 10,000 Naira too. We are not too downhearted yet though and determined to win through in the end.

I have been asked if I would write a review for the St. George's Day celebration dinner. This year it is going to be held in a friend's house in Ikeja. The Airport Hotel where we normally used to hold it is just too awful nowadays; too expensive and seems to have gone totally 'bush.' So far I have written the review after the fashion of the television show 'Not the Nine o'Clock News.' We don't have many aspiring actors here at the moment and no one wants to learn any lines but at least that way, some of the scenes can be read from a script. I've got some of the chaps doing a Morris dance in one scene and I have to say they have made it look absolutely hilarious. Brian has agreed to play the part of Lady Diana Spencer in an interview with 'Prince Charles' when they announced their engagement and another friend is playing the part of Barbara Cartland who will be singing a song in her bath about becoming part of the Royal Family now! It is quite funny so I hope it goes down well! Sadly it is on the same night that Sally and Nick have to return to school. Time is going far too quickly as it always does when they are here on holiday.

Will close now and hope that you all had a lovely Easter break. Will write again soon.

Lots of love to you and all the family.

As Always,

Maureen, Brian Sally and Nick.xxx

We had to move out of the Pfizer house the following week and kind friends Colin and Jan said we could move in with them until we found something for ourselves. They had just returned to Ikeja having been away for a few years and Colin had started with a new company so they hadn't fully settled in themselves yet. They were extremely kind to us and we finally ended up staying with them for nine weeks while Brian was trying to get import licences and letters of credit set up with the Government. Along with all the hassle that came with that, we now had to sort out another car and a house of some sort for us to live in.   We were running around like headless chickens. Everywhere was so expensive and with no money coming in it proved impossible for us to find anywhere reasonable enough to rent. Brian did get a new car, an Audi GLS100 which looked very smart, and arrived on his birthday in May   It was another white one though, and that was a very popular colour with the robbers for some reason so we had bright green flashing and Agri Products written all over it in an effort to make it more conspicuous. It looked like 'Starsky and Hutch's' car when it was finished! We also had an extra security device put on it which was a 'cut-off' switch that meant that you couldn't start the engine without knowing how to find and operate the switch. You just had to remember to flick the switch every time you turned off the engine and then if you were stopped by robbers, you had to run like hell into the bush and hide, before they discovered that they couldn't start it again!

It was a very frustrating time for Brian and the falling dollar also hit us hard which didn't help our cause either. The civilian government, which had been elected in 1979 with Shehu Shagari as Head of State was quickly losing a grip on the Country's rapidly declining finances. The price of oil fell and the newly appointed government was accused of massive corruption   We just couldn't seem to make any headway with the new Agri-Products business. President Shagari eventually declared the Country bankrupt and issued an overnight ban on the importation of new materials into Nigeria. Our business was totally reliant on the importation of ingredients essential for the manufacture of quality animal feedstuffs, i.e. grain, vegetable and animal-sourced protein and vital micro-ingredient supplements. This drastic and fatally flawed decision to stop import licences affected all industries, not only those involved in the Agricultural development. Thus, within a short time span, it resulted in the downfall of a Civilian government and the re-instatement of Military Rule under the auspices of General Obasanjo. We decided that we should go back to UK and Brian would 'commute' in and out from there. This meant that he was away in Nigeria for quite long periods of time, and then spending frustrating weeks back in the UK while waiting for

Government officials in Nigeria to get their act together. Nigeria didn't grow anything much except peanuts and guinea corn and the peanut industry was already in serious decline. It was a catastrophe for us when they banned the importation of grain. We had only managed to get one shipment through before that, for which we didn't get any payment until a couple of years later.

Sally had secured her first job, working as a bi-lingual secretary for a record company in UK. Nick was in his final two years at boarding school and I went back to College for a two year course to study Beauty Therapy. Brian, meanwhile was still travelling to and from Nigeria and his office in London. We were living on a shoestring. We felt that it was essential to keep Nick at school so that he could finish his education but Brian was only drawing his expenses from the business and things were getting a bit desperate. The most frustrating thing was playing the waiting game. You couldn't get through all the red tape and even though Nigeria desperately needed imported products, it just wasn't happening. Reluctantly, he had to wind the business up in 1984 and asked the Nigerian chairman to keep it 'on hold' until the Government either had a change of heart or a change of President.

I was working at a Beauty Salon in Walton on Thames by that time and Nick had finished school and secured a place at Kingston College studying Graphic Design.

Meanwhile, the new capital city of Nigeria was actually going ahead and was now being developed in Abuja, central Nigeria. An engineering company in the UK approached Brian to ask if he would be interested in working for them back in Nigeria where they were hoping to build a new hospital and eye clinic in Abuja. Brian knew 'the ropes' so to speak and had years of experience dealing with the authorities, and they needed someone who could be out there to organise everything for them. They were just waiting for the appropriate licences to be granted before they could go ahead with the plans. It meant another few frustrating and anxious months of waiting before he finally went back to Lagos in November 1985. He reported back to us that the new capital city was growing fast with new hotels, businesses, government buildings and all the infrastructure well under way. It was quite miserable for the men to be out in Nigeria on their own at any time but particularly when you didn't have your own place and had to rely on friends or 'bush' hotel accommodation for months at a time. We hated these long separations and so whenever Brian had the chance of getting me a ticket to join him, I went out for a few weeks. I enjoyed getting back into playing golf and bridge again and meeting up with the few expatriate friends who were still 'hanging on in there'!

In March 1986 Brian had gone back for a very important meeting with the Minister of the Federal Capital Abuja, one Major General Mamman Jiya

Vatsa. He was also a member of the Supreme Military Council and a personal friend from schooldays of the new President, Major General Ibrahim Babangida, who had recently come to power in August 1985 in a palace coup against Major General Buhari. Everyone was excited about the prospects of at last getting the appropriate licences and letters of credit that were required to enable the building of the hospital and clinic to start. Brian arranged for me to join him at the end of March. He was staying at a house on the G.Cappa Estate in Ikeja that had been rented by the company. Funnily enough, it was the same house that several of our friends had lived in during their time in Nigeria in the 1970s so it was familiar to us but in a sadly neglected state, as now it was only being used as temporary rented accommodation and had therefore been furnished extremely sparsely by the Nigerian landlord. There were no home comforts whatsoever and another couple of bachelors who were out in Nigeria working for the same company were also living there. The steward had been left to his own devices and the house and garden were in a rather dirty and unkempt state. It was not how it used to be and Brian felt very uncomfortable being there.

Unbelievably, in another incredible twist of fate, Brian learnt that Major General Vatsa had been executed on March 5th following a military tribunal conviction for treason associated with an abortive coup against his friend, Babangida. It appears that in December 1985 over a hundred military personnel were arrested for allegedly plotting to overthrow the four-month government of Babangida. Selected cases were put forward for tribunal. Apparently, it had been rumoured that Vatsa had wanted to be the next President and he had been accused of financing the plot to oust Babangida, which Vatsa strenuously denied. They had been childhood friends and former classmates since secondary school but it was thought that the rivalry between them had motivated the plot. Vatsa was accused of giving 10,000 Naira to two other officers, which he maintained to the end was to be used for the development of farming in the country and not for financing a coup which would have needed considerably more than a mere 10,000 Naira. The other two officers finally confessed that they had eventually used the money for expenses and not for farming but Babangida was not to be swayed and so along with Vatsa and many other officers at the time who were accused of treason, they were all taken out and shot.

This left Brian high and dry yet again until a new minister was elected and negotiations had to begin all over again. On the 14th April, Brian and his colleague had finally secured an appointment to meet with the new minister in Abuja. They needed to get a 'letter of award' from the minister in order for the development of the hospital and clinic to go ahead. It had taken a great deal of negotiation to get to this point and it was to be a very important meeting that would ensure the future success of the company.

CHAPTER 19 - APRIL 1986

G.Cappa Estate
Ikeja
LAGOS STATE
Nigeria

April 21st. 1986

My Dearest All
        Hope everyone in the family are fit and well.
We are fine here.   It is really stiflingly hot at the
moment and we are all desperate for some rain.   We
had the last storm at the end of March when we had a
fun weekend at the beach in the Dunlop chalet with
friends, Clive and Yvonne.   Clive is the Technical
Director of Dunlop here but they will be moving on
shortly to Trinidad and Tobago.   Sounds exciting
doesn't it?   Anyway, a few friends, mostly 'bachelors'
or chaps who are out here on their own, because their
wives have gone home, went across to Tarkwa Bay for
the weekend, including their Great Dane dog 'Raj'!
He is a beautiful dog and didn't seem to mind the trip
in the boat across the lagoon in the slightest.   We all
had great fun and slept that night on our sun-beds

under mosquito nets on the veranda, after having had a great barbecue and plenty of beer. We also had a Japanese friend with us, whom we all call 'Shogun' as his real name is unpronounceable. Shogun had prepared some fish as a starter for us, and it was raw! We were all a bit suspicious at first but he assured us that it was really fresh and when it had marinated for a while and was ready, we tried it and it was surprisingly quite delicious.

That night we had a terrific storm and we all got soaked through so we hardly got any sleep but apart from the fiercely biting mosquitos and sandflies, it all turned out to be quite hilarious. That was the last rain we have had to date and although it cleared the air for a few hours in the early morning, it turned out to be even hotter afterwards.

Brian and I have just got back from what you might call a' fairly adventurous trip' up to Abuja, a town which is being developed right now as the new capital city of Nigeria. Brian and his colleague Paul had to go up there for a meeting with the new Minister of the Federal Capital and so they decided to drive, partly so that I would be able to go along as well. Unfortunately, the first part of the 'adventure' turned out to be a disaster from the word 'go'! It started on the Sunday night. Brian and I had spent a lovely day at the beach with some friends, ending up with a Chinese meal at The Mandarin Restaurant and went off to bed for an early night, so we would be ready for a 5-30 am start the next morning. There is another chap staying with us in the house at the moment who is based in Calabar. He is only a young man, about 25 years old I would guess, and Paul had taken him down to Lagos for a bit of night-life, as Calabar is somewhat remote! Some time after midnight we were awoken by a frantic ringing of the doorbell. It was Paul. Apparently they had been involved in an accident on their way home on the 'infamous' Ikorodu road and the car wouldn't go, so Brian had to get up and go and tow them back in with the Range Rover. He was not amused as you can imagine, as it was after 3 o'clock when he finally got back to bed. In spite of that, we were up bright and early a couple of hours later with the car packed up, all ready to go but our Nigerian driver didn't turn up. At 6am, a man arrived to say that Sunday, the driver, had taken his wife to hospital as she was producing a child! So that was that, we had to set off on our own. It is normal here these days to have a Nigerian driver with you so he can take care of the car and guard it while you are not in it, even if he doesn't drive it all the time.

Brian set off driving with Paul in the front, still asleep and me in the back. We had a fairly uneventful journey until about midday when we had our first puncture! Fortunately we happened to be driving through a small bush village at the time and we saw a hut with tyres outside. Normally this means that whoever lives there repairs tyres. I must mention here that tyres are almost impossible to get hold of in Nigeria at the moment. Indeed, when Brian first flew out on this tour he brought a couple of tyres with

279

him because they are so scarce. Anyway, a small boy came out of the hut and jacked the car up and took the wheel off. He said that he could repair it, so rather than use our spare tyre with the prospect of such a long drive still ahead of us, Brian said to go ahead. He was highly amused at first to see the way he did it and wanted to take a photograph but they still have a certain fear of camera lens pointing at them so the boy wasn't very keen. Apparently, there were three holes in the inner tube, so the boy got a piece of raw rubber and cut off three pieces which he placed over the holes. He then lit a fire and tried to heat seal the raw rubber in place on the inner tube. This was a slow process and took a couple of hours, with Brian by this time getting more and more impatient and sceptical about what he was doing. As it was the middle of the day, it was also unbearably hot. I was standing by the car under a large golf umbrella trying to stay in the shade until we discovered a small hut nearby that sold drinks and food. We went across to it and a woman, who was dozing on the veranda under the shade of a tree, invited us to sit down with her while her daughter brought out some beer for us! The beer was warm and tasted horrible, but at least it was a drink and by this time, we were gasping for some liquid refreshment. The place was thick with flies and they were crawling all over us, sticking to our eyes, noses and lips as we tried to drink. The madame saw that I was troubled by them and called again for her daughter who came and splashed kerosene all over the floor and around our feet. You can imagine how much that enhanced the taste of the warm beer! It didn't really keep the flies away for long either, as they were soon back crawling all over us again. The woman then unwound her long head tie and proceeded to flick it in my direction. I found that to be a fairly nerve-racking experience as I wasn't quite sure what she was doing at first and thought that I was either going to be whipped with it or have the beer spilt all over me. Once I realised what she was trying to do though, I have to say that she was extremely skillful with it because even though it came perilously close to my face every time, it never actually touched me, or the beer, once! They also put on some very loud Nigerian Highlife music to entertain us, which gave cause for the local police officer to come along to find out what was going on! As time went on, they then offered to prepare a meal for us using their local delicacy, 'grass cutter' which is a bush meat that they eat and looks like an extremely large rat. Even though we were hungry by this time, we politely declined!

Meanwhile, Brian and Paul kept going back to see how the tyre repair was progressing. The boy had used blades of grass to poke through the holes so he could see where they were and apparently had even ended up stitching part of it at one point! We didn't hold out much hope! Anyway, finally it was ready and after some haggling over the price, we set off again, only progressing 5 kilometers down the road before the whole tyre blew out! This time there was an enormous hole in the tread as well and as we were on a *deserted stretch of road at this point, Brian and Paul had to change the wheel themselves after all. Normally this would have been a fairly simple operation, but the temperature was well over 100°F and both the car and the road surface were too hot to touch, so it became a major operation. I was standing with my umbrella again, trying to hold it over them to give them as much shade as possible and at the same time, trying to be conspicuous as a warning for the enormous tanker trailers that came thundering past at a murderous rate of knots, making us all periodically dive for cover to the edge of the bush before we got mown down. We finally got back on the road again with our fingers firmly crossed as we still had about another 200 miles to go.*

The total journey to Abuja from Ikeja is about 488 miles. Luck was not on our side that day I'm afraid, as some miles further on, we started to experience an enormous vibration which shook the whole car. We couldn't think what it was, so limped on slowly until we came to a small town where we stopped and asked where we could find a mechanic. We were directed to this place where we were asked to park over a large hole in the ground which the 'mechanic' then jumped into, as this was his 'inspection pit!' After much 'umming' and 'aahing' and scratching of heads, nobody seemed able to find out what was wrong, so Brian decided to keep going slowly in spite of the horrible vibrations that by now were making our teeth rattle! We were within about 50 miles of Abuja when the car got so bad that it became difficult to control on the road so when we were passing through a small village Brian drew up in front of another hut that was displaying old tyres outside. We were immediately surrounded by hoards of people and children who had obviously never seen a Range Rover before and apparently not many white people either! They chattered excitedly, pointing and laughing at us before one man stepped forward, having plucked up his courage before saying 'Ah Baturi!' which means white man. 'Good morning' (although it was evening by this time)! 'Why do you do?' which I thought was very amusing but quite brave of him all the same. Just as Brian was trying to enquire of somebody where we might find another mechanic, an ominous hissing sound drew our attention to the fact that the spare tyre they had fitted was now rapidly deflating! Well, that was it. No more spares. Another small boy was called and when he finally managed to get the wheel off and took the inner tube out, we discovered what the vibration had been, the inner tube was totally in half and had obviously just been flapping around inside the tyre.

We simply had to get to Abuja that night as the meeting with the Minister was at 10-30 the next morning. If we had had the driver with us, we could have left him with the car and gone on ourselves by taxi or some other transport but it just wasn't safe to leave the car on its own, as we would never have seen it again, so when a short time later, a taxi just happened to pass by, Paul flagged it down and it was decided that he would go to the nearest town which was just South of Abuja and try to buy a new tyre. We knew that this would be an almost impossible task as Range Rover tyres, or indeed any tyres are well nigh impossible to find. It was our only hope though, so off he went and Brian and I settled down in the car for a long wait. It was still unbearably hot and we were all sticky and dirty from the long journey. Thankfully, we had a little fruit and some water left so we weren't too badly off.

Brian was just trying to have a snooze when suddenly a tremendous wind blew up swirling all the red laterite dust around us, blinding and stinging eyes and skin and sending all the children, who were still curiously standing around gazing at us in the car, rushing for cover. We quickly closed all the windows and boot, and sitting in the car prayed that it wouldn't be blown off the jack, when the storm hit us with tremendous ferocity. The rain was torrential, it just sluiced down, obliterating everything for miles around. The skies were dark and the hot wind howled around us. The only good thing was that the jack held firm and when the storm finally petered out, the rain had at least cooled everything down.

Eventually, Paul returned and amazingly, (and at enormous expense, the equivalent of £70) had managed to buy an inner tube. It was dark by this time but the taxi driver, with the promise of yet more money, pointed his headlights at our car while they fixed it back on. After settling up yet another unexpected bill, we set off again. We travelled on for no more than 3 miles before we had yet another 'blow out!' We just couldn't believe it.

It was pitch dark in the 'bush.' The moon hadn't yet risen and the only light came from the headlights as we crawled along the tarmac strip that ran down the middle of the rough road. A huge MAN Diesel 16240 lorry towing an equally long trailer blasted his strident, blaringly loud, air-horn, forcing us off the metal strip onto the laterite as he thundered past us at enormous speed. All went quiet again, save for the low revs from the engine of the Range Rover and the sounds of the hot tropical night that drifted in through the open windows. Brian was driving very slowly. We had no more spare tyres with us. We should have been off the road and in our hotel long before dark. If it hadn't been for all the punctures we had experienced on the way we would have been. So we couldn't stop. It definitely isn't safe to be driving here on the roads at night. Highway robberies are commonplace and reports in the newspapers every day tell stories of people who have been held up at gunpoint, robbed, and in some cases, hacked to death by the felons if they tried to defend themselves. The robbers, who then mysteriously disappear into the night, never to be found or brought to justice, just continue, unhindered, with their ghastly 'trade.' We were bumping along on what was left of the tyres, running on the rim of the latest punctured one by this time. The atmosphere in the car was really tense, nobody spoke, as mile after slow mile we kept

285

trundling along hoping and praying that surely, nothing worse could possibly befall us this night.

But it did. Suddenly, out of the darkness ahead, a light started flashing at us indicating that we should pull over to the side of the road. Brian had no option but to continue driving slowly towards it. The light kept on flashing, insistently trying to direct us off the road. Brian wouldn't stop because there was only dense bush on either side of us and who knows what dangers might have been lurking in there. As we drew alongside the light, a man clad only in a loin cloth jumped out and started to jog alongside the car. My mouth went dry, and my heart started to pound loudly in my chest. Even in the heat of the tropical night I broke out into a cold sweat and started to shake with fright. We could only see the whites of his eyes as he stared in at us through the open windows. Then he spoke "Good evening Baturi' he said. "I go pass you on the road. I see you are in trouble. I wait for you now!' Brian kept on driving as fast as he dared to go. The man continued to jog along beside us as he demanded "Where are you going Baturi?' "We have to get to Abuja tonight' said Brian. 'Aaha! You no go get dere dis night' said the man. My heart beat even faster. "Make you go come with me now' he said. "I be the Chief of the village dere. You go come with me now now and I go help you.' We looked over to where he was pointing and saw the glow of firelight deep in the bush. What were we to do? It was becoming obvious that we would never make it to Abuja due to the state of our vehicle. "Can you get us a taxi or transport of some kind?' asked Brian. "Yes, yes, you go come with me now and I get you taxi' the man said. With that, he darted across the road in front of the car and ran down a cutting through the bush, heading towards the light from the fire. "Shall we follow?' asked Brian. We didn't have much choice. Better to go and see what was in the village than to spend the night on a deserted road miles from anywhere where we could have been waylaid by robbers, or worse. We turned off the road and bumped down a rough track, following the man until we drew up in a clearing, where the fire was burning brightly. The fire was surrounded by a ring of thatched mud huts. We drew up in front of one and the Range Rover was almost as big as the hut. This was the village! Nobody else was around but the sound of our vehicle arriving soon brought curious faces peering out of the doorways, lit up, like burnished copper from the reflected glow of the fire. Several men came over to have a closer look at us. The man we had followed was speaking rapidly and making excited gestures to the other men who now surrounded our car. We could not understand what they were saying as it was in their own tribal language. My fears grew stronger. What was going to happen to us now? Terrible thoughts crowded through my mind. What were we even doing here? Our children were in England! They might never find out what had become of us. We might never be found. Would I be tied up and raped? Would they hack us all to death with machetes?

The man went into his hut and dispatched a small boy, supposedly to rouse the taxi driver. While we waited nervously, he produced his business card and by the light of a candle we read that he was 'Umaru Musa. General contractor, Building construction, Suppliers of building materials such as Gravels, Sand, Planks, Stones, Laterites, Culverts, Cement, Food-stuff, Uniforms, Furnitures, Clearing of Site, and Transportation'! With our mood lightening somewhat, we waited. Surprisingly, after a while, the boy returned in a beat-up old car with a driver. We quickly took all our luggage, plus the spare wheel, that had also had a puncture earlier, and piled it all into the taxi. Musa said he would guard the Range Rover until we came back for it the next day. We had our doubts but frankly, by this stage I was beginning not to care about what happened to the car. We all thanked him and got into the taxi ready to go.

Suddenly the taxi driver started to rant and rage. We couldn't understand what he was saying as it was in his own language. We had agreed on a price, after some haggling, for him to take us to Abuja, but Musa said he wanted the money before he set off. Brian refused. The shouting grew louder and more aggressive. I was getting more frightened in the back seat while the argument continued. After a while, Musa told us that the driver wanted another man to come with us as he was afraid to come back on his own from Abuja after he dropped us off. We had to agree as we were all just about at the end of our tether by this time and ready to agree to almost anything in order for us to get going. Finally another man joined us and as Paul was in the front seat of the taxi, this other man squeezed into the back seat next to me. The smell of musk in the car was rank. It was the smell of their fear. Let alone ours!

The taxi driver finally set off at enormous speed but instead of turning back onto the main road, he turned left down another bush track. Brian and Paul both yelled at him 'Hey where the .... do you think you are going?' He continued down the rough bush track at about 60 miles per hour jolting us all around as he hit the pot holes at what seemed like enormous speed. This time, I was convinced our end had come. I clung to Brian literally shaking. The driver and this other guy were now taking us deeper into the bush, I was terrified that they were going to rob us and hack us to death. He suddenly slewed to a halt in front of another hut, blaring his horn all the while. I really thought then, this is it. This is the end. Black figures ran out towards us in the pitch dark, shouting excitedly..........

Suddenly someone ran up with a large Jerry can full of petrol and started pouring it through a funnel into the car! Phew! What a relief! In no time, off we went again and he drove as if the wrath of God was upon him. I didn't dare look but fortunately we didn't meet anything else on the road and eventually we arrived in Abuja.

The story didn't end there, however. We had been led to understand that one of the brand-new hotels that are being built up there was now open, but when we got there, it wasn't even finished and certainly wasn't open. Back we went to the only other hotel in Abuja that was operational only to be told that it was full. There was no power anywhere either so we just didn't know where to go next. The taxi driver was no help. He just wanted to go back home. We persuaded him to take us back to the new hotel to see if we could at least sleep in the lobby or something. When we got there we found that it really wasn't possible and we couldn't even get inside as it was all boarded up and very secure. If we had been in our own car at least we could have stayed in that. The taxi driver was getting increasingly more irate with our demands to take us backwards and forwards. He was also demanding more and more money. There was only one thing to do, and that was to go to the Camp where the Dutch company who were building the Hotel were living. Brian had been accommodated there once before when he had had the same problem in that there had been no room at the hotel but he really didn't want it to look as if he was taking advantage of their previous hospitality. Anyway, there was nothing else for it, either we slept on the roadside or Brian swallowed his pride and went and asked if they could help us out again. The taxi driver refused to take us any further and so we ended up walking to the camp, in the inky blackness of the night, carrying our bags and wheeling a shredded tyre in front of us.

No words will ever be adequate enough to express our deep gratitude for the kindness that those Dutch people from the Bredero camp showed to us that night, or indeed for the next two nights that they insisted we stayed with them. Once the nightwatchman at the gates finally understood our plight and went to rouse somebody in the camp, they took us in and were absolutely wonderful. You can't and never will believe or understand how good that first ice-cold beer tasted, how warm the friendship towards us was, when they welcomed us into their bar. Who were these mad English travellers who had been on the road for 15 hours, turning up at dead of night, dirty, bedraggled, hungry and tired and in my case, very frightened, wheeling a shredded tyre? It didn't seem to matter. They were amazing.

Just a quick comment here about how inferior the British seem to have become in their dealings with Nigeria at the moment. Abuja is a whole new Capital City which is being built here and not one major British contractor is playing a part in it. The Dutch, the Germans, the Italians, and the French, all have enormous building contracts. The Bredero company bring in all their own staff along with prefabricated houses which are all fully furnished and kitted out with everything they will require in the kitchens, bathrooms, bedrooms, etc and for the bachelors they have smaller ones which have just one room and a bathroom. They have a central restaurant, a general store, a television room, a laundry, a general bar and lounge area which is rather like a club, a beautiful swimming pool with an outside bar area, tennis courts and a skittle ally, and a large barbecue area. They also use two of the larger houses for their schools for the children and bring in their own teachers. The continental people all insist on this before they move their staff in to do the work. The Brits, however, in Lagos, just move in to existing houses, which they normally have to repair and maintain, pay exorbitant rents to Nigerian landlords, have to put up with existing power and water supplies which are practically non-existent now and try to live on the meagre produce that is available in the shops at the moment. British teachers are no longer allowed to teach in the schools unless there are no Nigerians available to teach certain subjects. It all boils down to the language. Qualified teachers in Nigeria all speak English but the standard is so low, hence the reason we have to send our children back to UK for their education.

Anyway, back to Abuja. That night, after we had been fed and watered, we were given a separate bachelor cabin each, with glorious air conditioning, comfortable beds and clean sheets, which only two hours previously we thought we would never ever see again. It was wonderful. The next morning, one of the wives who happened to be British came over to greet me and was extremely friendly. She had her husband's car and driver at her disposal and took me to see the local market, which I noted was so much cleaner than Lagos. Next, she took me all round

292

Abuja to show me the new buildings, roads and hotels that are being built. She was a qualified quantity surveyor herself so knew all the builders, even though she is not working here, as she has two small children, but her husband was one of the top men in Bredero. I had a conducted tour round all the big new hotels that are being built, the Sheraton, and the Hilton among them. I've never seen anything like it in Nigeria before and have to say, was most impressed. Meanwhile, Brian and Paul had been given a car and driver to take them to their meeting with the new Minister and were asked to go back again the next day. A lovely English guy called John who is head of the mechanical engineering department for Bredero, sent his driver plus one of his own tyres from one of his trucks to bring back the Range Rover for us. John had written a letter to Musa, authorising him to release the car. The driver returned saying that Musa refused to release the car to anyone except to the Baturi. So Brian had to go himself and pick it up later on. It was really very comforting to know that it was still there, even more so to find that he really was 'guarding it' and it quite restored our faith in Nigerians to find that Musa was not actually expecting huge sums of money for having looked after it for us. In fact, when Brian asked him what he owed, he said it was not necessary. Of course Brian gave him some money but it is well known that the Range Rover is worth N52,000 in Nigeria at the moment and we could easily have seen the last of it that night.

We couldn't get any more tyres for the car and so John fitted four of his own tyres for us to be able to drive back to Lagos with. The sheer generosity of this man was outstanding. You simply cannot get tyres here at the moment and to lend four precious tyres for three strangers to drive nearly 500 miles on was quite incredible to us. Neither would the Dutch people allow us to set off back to Lagos the following afternoon after Brian had seen the Minister again. They said that after 7-30 in the morning, it was too late to set off anywhere! The following morning, when we did set off at 7-15am, we found that the husband of Chris, the English girl, had organised the kitchen to prepare sandwiches for us plus a full loaf of bread to take back to Lagos. They bake their own bread every day as they have their own flour flown in, whereas we can't even buy flour in Nigeria at the moment. Fortunately, we had a safe journey back to Lagos, it was long, but without incident. But guess what, when we got into the drive and were just unloading the car, a tyre suddenly started to hiss..... and down it went!

What an experience! Another one to join the long list of Nigerian or African 'happenings'! There's never a dull moment I must say.

The scenery in the North was quite spectacular in parts. There was one place where an enormous rock just rose out of the ground. The locals say it is sacred and is filled with water! I doubt it, but in any event, they won't let you get near it. It is known as Zuma Rock. I have taken some photos through the car window, so I hope they come out well as it is quite extraordinary.

While I have been writing this, the steward Augustine has just come in to show me that he has baked some bread. He is very proud. Apparently, he found flour in the market today and some yeast. He had to pay N9.oo for a bag of flour so of course I repaid him. That is nearly the equivalent of £9 at the moment! I just don't know how these poor people can afford to live here. They go without more and more and exist on less and less. He has seven children too. Mind you that's his fault!

Hope all goes well for all of you and that everyone is fit.
Won't be long until we are home now, though I don't know the exact date yet. Me, definitely before the end of May but Brian, not sure, as it is crucial for him to see that this contract for the hospital goes through.
Will close now and send

All our love to you all.
As Always,

Brian and Maureen. xxxx

CHAPTER 20 - LEAVING

That was effectively the last letter I wrote home from Nigeria.

Strange things began to happen within the company that Brian was now working for. After our trip to Abuja, Paul went to Calabar to inform his friend Mark of likely progress being made, but couldn't find him anywhere so flew back to Lagos to report his disappearance to Brian. They decided they had better go and report it to the British High Commission. It transpired that Mark, had suddenly been taken to Apapa, and placed under house arrest in the Military camp there, which was adjacent to the infamous Kiri Kiri prison. It appeared that he had been throwing his weight around at his squash club in Port Harcourt, with two Nigerian members who turned out to be high ranking military personnel. Mark, a rather brash and inexperienced young man, had reportedly been bragging about his connection to Madame Vatsa, for whom he continued to work as manager of their poultry farm even after her husband had been shot. The Nigerians took exception to his remarks, and thinking that he might have had something to do with the suspected coup, immediately had him arrested.

Brian went to the British High Commission again to try to plead Mark's case. Paul then disappeared without telling Brian or anyone else where he was going. I answered the phone at the house one day when Brian was again at the High Commission in Lagos, and it was a Major from the Nigerian Army who began asking me all sorts of questions. During the course of the conversation, it became obvious that our phone was either being 'tapped' or else we were being watched, as he asked why Brian was at the High Commission and where his colleague Paul had gone to. We were having to take food down to Mark in Apapa as he wasn't being given anything that he could eat. It was also necessary for us to send to UK for copies of all Mark's documents with proof of his work permits and visas and because the post was so slow it was taking a long time for these to come back to us. From then on, we didn't use the phone at the house and had to go to a neighbour when we wanted to make any calls.

After all our happy years in Nigeria, it was a sad sign of the times. There had always been corruption on a massive scale in the country but this was now getting beyond belief. Pfizer had never tolerated or succumbed to any form of bribery or corruption and all their personnel had to sign papers every year to that effect. The directors of the company that Brian was now working for in London had obviously relied on the fact that General Vatsa would push their contract through in Abuja. Now it seemed that after his assassination, we were also being targeted for simply having had that contact.

Brian felt it would be safer for me to return to UK. He had never been party to any bribery in business and did not intend to start now. If the contract couldn't be awarded on a proper and fair basis, then he didn't want any part of it. He stayed on in Nigeria until Mark was released from prison. Paul, it turned out, had done 'a runner' and already returned to UK afraid he might become yet another innocent victim in a situation over which we had no apparent control. Brian finally came home in June that year and gave in his notice. It was a sad time for us all. When we had first arrived in Nigeria, the old regime had seemed respectful and grateful for the help the expatriate companies were giving to the nation after the dreadful Biafran war. Now, after oil had been discovered and indigenisation had taken place, greed and corruption had changed the mood of the younger generation and we no longer felt welcome or particularly safe in their country.

On my final journey home from Nigeria that day, as the plane took off and circled over Lagos I gazed down upon the now familiar scene for one last time. With tears in my eyes and a lump in my throat, my mind drifted back to the very first time I had seen that sight when we were coming in to land all those years ago. The excitement that the children and I were feeling then, as we looked forward to our new life that was about to begin on this vast continent of Africa.

I had many hours on that flight home to reflect upon our lives to this point. To think back over the last sixteen years, remembering all that had happened to us during that time. Some people had made fortunes in Nigeria, our fortune came, not from money, but from the wealth of experiences we shared; the fun, the laughter and the tears that we had along the way; the precious friendships we had forged and still hold dear in our hearts. The hard work, the many frustrations, the hardships that we all endured, the mountain of memories that remain; the sights, the sounds and the smell of Africa are deeply embedded in our souls. All these things have contributed to the making of a very rich period in our lives.

Our children had grown into young adults and thanks to their own experiences of life in and out of Nigeria were now able to lead independent and confident lives of their own.

We left Nigeria, as we had arrived, with just two suitcases in the hold, but with a renewed sense of anticipation tingling in our heads. For us, another new chapter of our lives was about to begin.

EPILOGUE

France
2016

Dearest Mum and Dad
If you are looking down on us now from somewhere up there, as I like to think you are, I just want to say thank you for keeping all those letters that I wrote to you from Lagos all those years ago.

The one that I first took out and started to read, brought back too many memories which I didn't feel able to face at the time.   I had only chosen to remember the good times, of which there were many, but when I finally decided to read them all, and match them up with all my old diaries, I felt that perhaps the time had come to tell the story.

We have four beautiful grandchildren now, all young adults and beginning to branch out into their own independent lives. They think nothing of travelling the world to explore exotic places these days.

I thought they may be interested one day to read about some of the life that we had led when we were young. (Even perhaps to know that we actually had a young life once upon a time!)

Times have changed so much since you were here.   You would not believe it if I tell you that most people now have mobile phones or tablets of their own. (Not the sort of tablets that you knew as medicine!) but small gadgets that are slim and portable enough to carry in pockets or bags, and on these, you can access the Internet which allows you to phone or connect to people around the world in seconds. You can even see the people as you talk to them if you wish.

How wonderful that would have been when we were in Lagos, instead of having to wait weeks for news of you. If we ever needed to talk to you, we had to drive all the way down to Lagos to the International Exchange to book a phone call to England, and sometimes wait for several hours before we were finally able to talk to you for just a few minutes. Don't ask me how the Internet works, I cannot begin to imagine as it is too amazing to get my head round. Suffice it to say, that all sorts of Satellites are now flying around in space and I think they bounce all these wonders back to Earth. The advance of technology today is simply incredible.

You can also get all the information you would ever need by typing the question on your phone or tablet. You can read the news from around the globe, although I'm not entirely sure if that is such a good thing as there are so many wars raging and so much suffering around the world that it can be quite depressing. Sometimes, ignorance was far less worrying!

Brian and I live a somewhat quieter life now in France, surrounded by acres of vines and small but beautiful old towns and villages. The climate is lovely, cold in Winter when we stay cosy by the wood burning stove but long hot Summers which enable us to spend much of our time outdoors.

Sally and Nick and their families are frequent visitors, as are many of our old friends. It is for them that I have written this book in the hope that they will enjoy the memories it has revived as much as we have.

THE END

ABOUT THE AUTHOR

Maureen was packed off to join her sister at boarding school in 1950. At a young age, she soon discovered that her obligation to write home on a weekly basis was no longer a chore, but a passion. Along with her writing, she also found a talent for dance, amateur dramatics and the arts.

After leaving school, Maureen completed a Foundation Year at The Manchester College of Art. She also performed regularly with Amatuer Dramatic Societies and in two series for the BBC's Children's Hour before finding work at the Oldham Repertory Theatre Company.

Maureen married Brian at the age of nineteen. During the early years of their marriage, his work saw them frequently moving around the UK, with their two small children, before Brian's posting in 1970 led them further afield - this time throwing them into expatriate life in West Africa.

Sixteen years of living in Nigeria clearly left a yearning to continue living 'abroad' as their next project took them 'across the water' to the Isle of Wight!

During the following fifteen years they bought a hotel and created a nursing home (another book perhaps?), before retirement brought a final move to France, where they now enjoy a somewhat quieter life.

19917779R00172

Printed in Great Britain
by Amazon